AMERICA'S #1 SALES COACH
TAMARA BUNTE

PROVERBS FOR SELLING

Mastering Sales
Through Prospecting, Referrals & Discipline

Diamond :)
Blessings

PEARHOUSE
PRESS
.COM

Proverbs for Selling
Mastering Sales Through Prospecting, Referrals and Discipline
by Tamara Bunte

Editorial Director: Dr. Larry Keefauver

Printed in the United States of America.

ISBN 978-0-9886721-6-1
LCCN: 2016950252

Published by Pearhouse Press, Pittsburgh, PA
www.pearhousepress.com

Contact...

tamarabunte
AMERICA'S #1 SALES COACH

To schedule Tamara to speak at your event, call:

704-247-8333

For more information, go to
www.TamaraBunte.com
www.ProverbsForSelling.com

This book is dedicated to the most important person in my life, my son, Jude

With his birth, God gave me beauty for ashes

Hope deferred makes the heart sick, but a longing fulfilled is a tree of life.
(Proverbs 13:12)

Table of Contents

Acknowledgments

I have been blessed with a family and team of coaches that are dedicated to my becoming the best version of myself. Pastor Cedric Maddox deserves special thanks for being my mentor and friend through all of life's curveballs and for challenging my God strategy to believe for more!

Scoobie Bunte, my precious little dog (first child) that patiently sat on my lap as I wrote this entire book and is an angel sent straight from heaven. She offers me unconditional love and approval of every word!

To Dale Carnegie and Tony Robbins for giving me the opportunity to study under their wisdom, and to my parents for encouraging me and supporting me when I needed it the most.

To all that have been a part of my journey, thank you for your support and love.

"The world ain't all sunshine and rainbows; it's a very mean and nasty place,
and I don't care how tough you are,
it will beat you to your knees and keep you there permanently if you let it.
You, me or nobody is going to hit as hard as life,
but it ain't about how hard you're hit,
it's about how hard you can get hit and keep moving forward.
It's about how much you can take and keep moving forward –
That's how winning is done.
Now, if you know what you're worth, go out and get what you're worth,
but you gotta be willing to take the hits and not be pointing fingers
saying you ain't where you wanna be because of him or her or anybody.
Cowards do that, and that ain't you. You're better than that."

– Sylvester Stallone, *aka* Rocky

Preface

I had just completed an hour presentation on the "Secrets of Selling" when a real estate agent came up to me and said, "All of the trainers out there tell me to call ten people a day and meet five new people. I've always wondered, who are the ten special people that I'm supposed to call and where do I meet five people a day? Your presentation gave me these answers. I always knew what to do, but I didn't know how to do it."

May I ask you some probing questions?

▶ *Does this sound like you or a team that you are leading or are part of?*

▶ *If I were to give you a referral and you called my friend three times and she didn't call you back, what would you say on the fourth voicemail?*

▶ *Do you know specifically how to get someone to return your phone call and, in turn, position yourself so that they are so excited to work with you that* ***they*** *invite you over for a meeting?*

▶ *What if we met eight months ago and you determined eight months later that I'm a viable lead? What do you say eight months later to get an appointment with me?*

▶ *Have you asked every person that bought your product or service from you in the last 6 months for a referral? Do you have a referral form?*

1

> ▸ *What customer relationship management system (CRM) do you use to follow up with your prospects? Does your system have a follow-up structure embedded into it? What do you say to earn their business?*
> ▸ *Do you call every lead five to twelve times a year? If so, how often do you call, how do you close someone that has no idea who you are or what you sell? Where on God's earth do you meet five people a day? Is it at a fast food restaurant at lunch time?*

Ask yourself, what is one skill that, if you were absolutely excellent at it, would help you increase your income the most? Is it prospecting? Obtaining referrals? Closing referral business? Or cold-calling? Who do you call after you've called all of the online leads you have, all of the referrals, and everyone in your basket full of business cards? Is sales success up to the sales and marketing department, your company name and location, or is it up to you?

In this book, I will challenge each person to participate in their own rescue and truly learn how to earn new business. It's not luck, and God doesn't have favorites. If we can learn from the best salesman on earth, Jesus, we might find that we can create a lot of business from very little. Jesus only had a few fish and a few pieces of bread, yet he multiplied it by thousands. Maybe with God's wisdom we can take what was meant to harm us, bad leads with no buying potential, and we can turn that around so that we can master the principles of prosperity.

Salespeople are typically very reactive. They are challenged with how to build a plan for prospecting and building new business. This book offers practical steps to successful prospecting, how to make even more money, how to get vertical referrals, and the classy techniques to grow your business. I will adjust your mindset to recognize that you and everyone essentially is a salesperson in some way or another and how to obtain the mindset of prosperity. I will answer common questions that professionals haven't found good answers to and teach you how to win over objections and cut through the outdated, regurgitated sales jargon that doesn't work today.

Proverbs for Selling provides an in-depth, soulful approach to renewing readers' spirits, fortifying their skillsets, and empowering them to improve their sales strategies to work smarter and more productively. This book will give you a renewed spirit so you can be confident and excited about selling.

It's time for you to discover the principles to make millions!

Most people don't like what they do, struggle financially, are not in a passionate relationship, and are not physically fit, but I'm interested in the ones that are. I'm a hunter of excellence. This book extracts the wisdom of the book of Proverbs from the Bible and shows anyone how to strive for more and actually obtain it. Discover the disciplines that empower you to take your sales career to a new level.

Whether you are a top sales professional wanting to raise your game or the chief executive officer wanting to influence a team of people to become the best version of themselves, this book will merge the gap between theory and execution. Someone is always selling someone. The question is, are you selling people on why they should buy from you now? Or are they selling you on their excuses as to why not to buy? Learn to master your emotions and control the sales cycle to win people to your way of thinking.

Sales professionals today can't rely on marketing, the economy, or anything but their own strategy and implementation of it. Success is about consistent, intelligent action. You must know who to call, when to call, what to say and, most importantly, how to lead someone to make a decision to buy.

In this book you'll learn how to:

▸ Ask for referrals and obtain referral business – the classy way.

▸ Make cold-calling (making new friends) simple, and learn how to be awesome at it.

▸ Get past the gatekeeper, ask questions that establish your value, and earn even more business.

▸ Make the sales process simple and create systems to condition yourself for action.

▸ Master Prospecting – How to get the right prospects knocking on your door.

▸ Overcome setbacks and learn how to participate in your own rescue.

▸ Act and grow rich. Become a master of execution.

Ready? Let's learn, master, and put into daily practice these *Proverbs for Selling!*

> *Do you see someone skilled in their work? They will serve before kings; they will not serve before officials of low rank.* (Proverbs 22:19)

INTRODUCTION

Pro-Verbs: The Book of Wisdom

The Usefulness of Proverbs
To know wisdom and instruction,
To discern the sayings of understanding,
To receive instruction in wise behavior,
Righteousness, justice and equity;
To give prudence to the naive,
To the youth knowledge and discretion,
A wise man will hear and increase in learning,
And a man of understanding will acquire wise counsel,
To understand a proverb and a figure,
The words of the wise and their riddles.
(Proverbs 1:2-6)

W isdom is the application of knowledge. In the Old Testament, the word "wise" is used to describe people skillful in working with their hands. It's not something theoretical; it's very practical and affects every area of our lives. Have you ever met someone who knew everything, but didn't experience the fruit of that knowledge? This person is typically puffed up with pride telling others what to do, but not applying it to their own life. They may have acquired a great deal of knowledge, but have no understanding of how to apply it to their lives.

Knowledge is knowing the right thing to do; wisdom is actually doing it.

The book of Proverbs is our instruction manual for how to get knowledge and understanding, and then use godly wisdom to become truly "wise." It will help us define our values using godly principles to set proper priorities and develop our character. Following God's value system will bring order and purpose to our lives and give us discernment in making wise decisions. Choosing to follow wisdom's path will lead to the blessings God wants us to enjoy and will provide a sense of fulfillment to our lives.

Why do some people "know" what to do, but others actually "execute?"
Is it attitude or aptitude?
Why is there such a huge gap between the people who "know"
what to do, and those who actually do it?

Wanting to find the answers to these questions, I asked an audience of 200 real estate sales agents how many of them liked running. Ten people raised their hands. When I asked the remaining 190 participants how many of them ever do run even though they didn't like to, zero hands went up. It dawned on me that if someone doesn't like making Cold-Calls, they simply won't do them, just like those who do not like running. However, those who like to prospect will want to get really good at it just like those who have decided they like running.

So, why do some people love to run while others do not? They simply have found reasons to support their choice and have found someone to give them strategies that make them love to do it. So, if we want to love to do what most people hate (like prospecting), all we have to do is find someone that loves doing it and learn to do what they do so successfully. The best way to get motivated is to be around someone that is already motivated. To be wise, we must think the thoughts of the wise ones, learn the disciplines that they possess, and practice until we master them.

Incline your ear and hear the words of the wise, and apply
your mind to my knowledge.
(Proverbs 22:17)

Proverbs tells us very clearly that hard work brings profits and that mere talk leads only to poverty. Wisdom teaches us how to use consistent *intelligent* action, not just work hard and hope to make more sales and money. Just because we're moving does not mean we're making progress. By learning how to be intentional and apply wisdom to our sales strategies, we become skilled in our work.

If we break the word Proverbs into two words, we have "Pro" and "Verbs." A verb is a word used to describe an action, state, or occurrence.[1] Therefore, the entire book of Proverbs is about applied knowledge, which is all about taking action. We must be pro-active in our efforts.

"Pro" + "Verbs" (Pro-Actions) = Wisdom

---

[1] © 2015 Merriam-Webster, Incorporated

Rich Man, Poor Man

Lazy hands make a man poor, but diligent hands bring wealth. (Proverbs 10:14)

There are three kinds of people discussed in Proverbs. The lazy person who never works but expects others to take care of them, the poor who need our help, and the diligent workers who acquire wealth.

The lazy person is mentioned at least seventeen times in Proverbs. These people are good at making excuses for not working, yet they complain because they live in poverty and hunger. They tend to have a know-it-all attitude and boast about how great they are, but when it comes to their paycheck they often live in the confines of poverty. A lazy person will always think they are doing more than they actually are. There may be lots of motion, but when it comes down to it there is really no progress.

There is a difference between being broke and being poor. Being broke is usually temporary for a salesperson as they wait for commission checks. It is the nature of the sales industry. Typically, poverty is caused by a poor mindset and is often based on emotions. A person who is emotionally overwhelmed by what they have to do may allow stress to paralyze them and therefore accomplish nothing.

If one can learn to master their emotions by letting their wise decisions dictate their actions, their emotions will tend to fall in line. Time, energy, money, and opportunity are wasted when emotions dictate choices and leisure and pleasure control a person's life. It constitutes emotional suicide versus emotional fitness.

Success is a choice, not a feeling, but many people's lives are ruled by their emotions rather than by their wise decisions.

The rich man is the self-disciplined, diligent worker. These are the people that play offense rather than playing defensive all the time. They push through the pain and make things happen.

Benjamin Franklin said, "Diligence is the mother of good luck." Proverbs 21:15 asserts, "The plans of the diligent lead to profit as surely as haste leads to poverty" (NIV). That plain assertion should prick the ears of all entrepreneurs and salespeople!

Diligent people seek knowledge and develop their skills. Too many people mistake knowledge for skill. Just because a person knows a lot does not mean they can execute a new strategy. A skill is developed when one has the attitude to learn something new, the motivation to obtain the needed knowledge, and then the determination to put what they have learned into practice. I believe in merging the gap between theory and execution. The only way to do that is to put knowledge into practice. Practice makes what we do over and over become a skill. If one practices procrastination, they will be skilled in it. Unfortunately, procrastination is not a high-paying skill.

A diligent person is not a procrastinator. They will decide what it is they need to learn, go after the knowledge they need, and then begin to develop their skill level through diligently practicing it. A sign of procrastination or laziness is when one is unwilling to measure their performance. "You can't manage what you don't measure." A procrastinator will always think they are doing more than they actually are.

As a door turns on its hinges, so does the lazy man on his bed.
(Proverbs 26:14)

If their goal is to make 1 million dollars next year, they will develop a plan and a skillset to reach that goal. By adding in more intentional, intelligent action, a salesperson can exceed their potential. If they choose to reach out to one new person a day to build their network five days a week, that's twenty new people that they now know. That's 240 new people/companies (prospects) in a year. If you are just average in sales, you will have a 6 percent closing ratio (that's bad), but still you will have fourteen new clients that you didn't have before. Let's face it, one dial a day takes less than ten minutes. If you are above average and have a 50 percent closing ratio, that's 120 new deals!

Diligent people are also self-disciplined, which is a key component of the Fruit of the Spirit.[2] They are careful not to incur debts they can't handle because they have learned, "The rich rule over the poor, and the borrower is servant to the lender" (Proverbs 22:7). Self-discipline includes not overextending by buying something with the anticipation of an upcoming sale. A sale is not a sale until the client signs on the dotted line and the check is in the bank. Too many sales professionals have lots in their pipeline, but don't realize that they have to replenish their pipeline while they are waiting for these payments to come in. It takes self-control to not indulge in instant gratification and spend money they do not yet have in hand.

---

[2] Galatians 5:22-23 says, "But the fruit of the Spirit is love, joy, peace, patience, kindness, goodness, faithfulness, gentleness, self-control; against such things there is no law."

The discipline here is to be in control of our finances rather than letting our finances control us. Thus, if we are in control of our prospecting efforts, we have more control over our finances.

Along these same lines is overcoming the destructive mindset that we aren't successful until we have a BMW, a big house, and other "stuff" we feel validates success. Self-discipline will help keep us from falling into the "**If** I make this amount of money, **then** I will be successful" mindset. The real measure of our wealth, according to John Henry Jowett, "is how much we'd be worth if we lost all our money." The byproduct of a disciplined sales career is enough money so that we can be in a position to lend and not borrow. I particularly like how the Bible tells us that we are to owe no one anything except to love each other.[3] The rich man will earn his keep and then use what he has been blessed with to bless others.

> *Indeed, we hear that some among you are leading an undisciplined and inappropriate life, doing no work at all, but acting like busybodies [meddling in other people's business]. Now such people we command and exhort in the Lord Jesus Christ to settle down and work quietly and earn their own food and other necessities [supporting themselves instead of depending on the hospitality of others].* (2 Thessalonians 3:11-12 AMP)

When we ask God to bless us, it means we are asking for His supernatural power to step in and help us. What we need to realize is asking God in faith that is not accompanied by action is ineffective just like skill and

---

[3] See Romans 13:8.

knowledge are of no use unless they are put into action. So, let's pray to be blessed financially and then let us be proactive and do our part. Sales is one of a few careers where we get to decide the size of our paycheck. Let's do our part and have a vision beyond the "stuff" and tap into what really can bring joy to our lives.

> **If you want to get really motivated, go to a local orphanage and pledge to feed those kids for a month. I guarantee you will exceed your quota that month!**

Wisdom from the Pro-Verbs

▸ Knowledge is knowing the right thing to do; wisdom is actually doing it.

▸ "Pro" + "Verbs" (Pro-Actions) = Wisdom

▸ Success is a choice, not a feeling, but many people's lives are ruled by their emotions rather than by their wise decisions.

▸ The discipline here is to be in control of our finances, which means controlling our prospecting efforts rather than letting our finances or distractions control us.

Ask Yourself...

▸ *Am I in control of my finances and prospecting efforts or are they in control of me?*

▸ *Do I really want to max out my potential? Do I know how?*

▸ *Am I willing to do what it takes to max out my potential?*

▸ *How can I do more to impact this world for the good by being blessed financially?*

Pro-Verb Action Steps:

Sales is one of a few careers where you get to decide the size of your paycheck. Will you choose to go big?

1. Describe what your maximum potential would look like.

2. List what you need to do to begin to max out your potential.

3. Evaluate how you handle your finances. Begin by listing things you have purchased in the last month and the last year that are not yet paid for. Set a goal from now on to not purchase "wants" that you do not have the money for. Begin to take control of your finances so they will not control you.

4. Begin to do more to impact your world by going to a local orphanage and pledge to feed those kids for a month.

A generous man will prosper; he who refreshes others will himself be refreshed. People curse the man who hoards grain, but blessing crowns him who is willing to sell. (Proverbs 11:25-26)

CHAPTER 1

The Seven Deadly Sins of Sales

There are things the LORD hates, seven that are detestable to him: haughty eyes, a lying tongue, hands that shed innocent blood, a heart that devises wicked schemes, feet that are quick to rush into evil, a false witness who pours out lies, and a man who stirs up dissension among brothers. (Proverbs 6:16-19)

When we talk about the seven deadly sins, they are usually seen as pride, greed, wrath, slothfulness, envy, gluttony, and lust. These are not only sins God hates, they are destructive in the world of sales as well. We will break these down into real-life scenarios so we can see how these sins infiltrate our work lives and why it's so important to avoid them at all costs.

1. Pride: As a Sales Sin, this refers to putting others down and talking negatively about the competition.

Pride is considered the most serious of the seven deadly sins. It is essentially believing we are better than others. It is excessive admiration of the personal self and leads to boasting. Pride leads to other sins and comes just before a fall.[4] The more pride the deeper the valley. There is a difference between confidence and pride. Confidence is being sure of what you know to be true; pride is boasting in that knowledge. As sales professionals, we can fall into pride by thinking we are better than our competition and putting them down to make our product/service look more superior. When we gossip, we are tapping into pride as well as an insecure way to make ourselves look better. We are **all** made in God's likeness and image, so no one is better than anyone else. Let's not attack a person but rather attack the facts. That way it never becomes the salesperson's fault or stirs up anger from a prospect.

> *A man's pride will bring him low, but a humble spirit will*
> *obtain honor.* (Proverbs 29:23)

2. Greed: As a Sales Sin, this refers to taking on debt or stealing.

Greed is also a sin of excess, but applies itself to a very excessive desire and pursuit of material possessions. It's all about wanting to acquire more for the sake of having more when we already have more than we need. Hoarding of material objects and wanting material goods more than the treasures stored up in heaven is a clear sign of greed. Greed can lead to other sins such as theft and robbery, especially by means of violence, trickery, or manipulation of authority. It can show up as stealing sales referrals or selling a product the customer does not need. Greed is about gaining more and manipulating the system for one's own selfish gain.

When I think of greed, I think of the movie *Wall Street*, where Michael Douglas tells us that greed is good and that greed motivates us to do more

---

[4] See Proverbs 16:18.

for the sake of more, which is, of course, off kilter. I've never seen a salesperson motivated by greed last longer than a few months.

3. Wrath: As a Sales Sin, this refers to losing your cool.

Wrath is otherwise known as intense anger. One of the laws of sales is to "never lose your cool," and I've learned this from experience. Anger can show up as sarcasm, which is hurting someone's feelings, stirring up strife, causing trouble, and then covering it up by saying, "I was only joking." Once we feed our anger or find reasons to justify why we should be upset, our anger will manifest in other ways such as impatience, revenge, selfishness, and other self-destructive behaviors. Anger that is internalized sometimes manifests itself as the main emotion leading to drug abuse and suicide. Depression is anger turned inward. To dispel wrath, we need to practice the discipline of forgiving the transgressions of others and leaving vengeance to God so we aren't tempted to lose our cool with our customers.

The customer is always right, even if they're wrong. We must not take a lost sale personally. You can never lose your cool, get angry, or make your prospect feel guilty for not buying or they will flee. We must take on the belief that eventually everyone will buy and never burn a bridge.

4. Slothfulness: As a Sales Sin, this refers to blaming others for our own lack of results.

Slothfulness is usually defined as physical and spiritual laziness. It is basically a failure to do things that one knows they should do. Evil exists when good men fail to act. In fact, James 4:17 says, "Anyone, then, who knows the good he ought to do and doesn't do it, sins" (NIV). I recently ran into a salesperson who lacked self-discipline and blamed the boss, the company, the company location, the marketing department, etc. for her poverty. I know for a fact the company offered to pay her for the time she needed to train and improve her skills and performance. She was not taking personal responsibility for her actions and was instead blaming everyone and everything she could instead of being grateful for the opportunity God had provided for her. What she failed to realize was that God had already put what she needed in place. She just had to step up and do her part. We all have to act on these gifts God provides for us. We already have the inner motivation, but we may just not be tapping into it.

I've never met an enthusiastic failure. We must take personal responsibly for our results; in essence, we must participate in our own rescue. Waiting for God to show up and save us from our laziness isn't a very good strategy. The question is, are we tapping into it?

5. Envy: As a Sales Sin, this refers to being jealous of someone else's success.

Envy, like greed and lust, is characterized by an insatiable desire. Envy is similar to jealousy in than there is a feeling of discontentment about their own level of success so they measure their current reality against someone else's status, abilities, or rewards. Sometimes it becomes easy to complain, thinking that someone doesn't deserve what they've received. Thinking we are smarter or better than a colleague who landed a big client sets us up for sin.

Where the sin gets into the mix is when the envious person also desires what others have and begins to covet it. Coveting moves people to try to steal something that is not theirs. It is also breaking one of the Ten Commandments, "Thou shalt not covet thy neighbor's house, wife, or possessions." We can appreciate what we have, water our own lawn, and watch it blossom instead of thinking the grass is greener in our neighbor's yard.

6. Gluttony: As a Sales Sin, this refers to being a workaholic.

Gluttony is defined as an overindulgence and overconsumption of anything to the point of waste.[5] Gluttony can be interpreted as selfishness; essentially placing concern for one's own interest above the well-being or interests of others. We can overindulge in good things and bad things. When working with sales professionals, it is called being a workaholic. These people may be overindulging like they would with any other food or drug to overcompensate for not wanting to face certain issues in their personal life. They work and work until they burn out. The opposite of gluttony is temperance. Too much of anything, even a good thing, is still too much.

7. Lust: As a Sales Sin, this refers to focusing on your commission over your customers' needs.

Lust is defined as an intense and uncontrolled desire.[6] It is usually thought of as uncontrolled sexual wants; however, the word was originally a general term for desire. Therefore, lust could include the uncontrolled desire for money, food, fame, or power. From a sales perspective, it usually shows up in the form of wanting the sales commission more than doing what is in the best interest of the customer. This becomes obvious when the salesperson's first question is, "When are you looking to buy?" Let's practice fulfilling the desires of our clients before our own. Pressure to reach sales goals can lead us to violate our own values rather than developing the discipline to continually fill our pipeline the right way.

In Dale Carnegie's book *How to Win Friends and Influence People*, he points out how important it is to see things from the other person's point of view. "You can close more business in two months by becoming

---

[5] © 2015 Merriam-Webster, Incorporated

[6] © 2015 Merriam-Webster, Incorporated

interested in other people than you can in two years by trying to get people interested in you."[7]

> *But each one must carefully scrutinize his own work [examining his actions, attitudes, and behavior], and then he can have the personal satisfaction and inner joy of doing something commendable without comparing himself to another.*
> (Galatians 6:4 AMP)

Stop Trying and Start Trusting

> *For where your treasure is, there your heart [your wishes, your desires; that on which your life centers] will be also.*
> (Matthew 6:21 AMP)

So, how do we move away from and conquer the pull of these seven deadly sins? Real motivation is having a goal to fulfill that is outside of oneself. God specifically tells us to put our money where our heart is, which should be in heavenly treasures, not earthly things. I know for certain that you will be blessed when you become a blessing to others. If you embrace your place and count the blessings that you do have, those blessings will start to multiply. Now you might be thinking, I don't have any blessings. Just look at how bad my situation is. Look at how unfair life has been to me! The prescription for your pain and lack is praise. Praise means the most when you feel like doing it the least.

Many of us were raised with the belief that life is supposed to be fair. I believe that people will reward me in business for helping them make

---

[7] http://www.brainyquote.com/quotes/authors/d/dale_carnegie

money, but yet it doesn't always happen that way. I expect people to be honest, trustworthy, and respectful, yet some only care about themselves and I find that they can and will take advantage of that. This used to make me very angry and bitter.

I had some people who really did me wrong and I just wanted to "get even" and have things turn out "fair." I wanted them to feel the way I felt; I wanted revenge. There was this root of bitterness in me that continued to grow as I kept replaying the wrongs that were done. Then I would imagine them getting just what they deserved. I lived in this angry, bitter, vengeful place for a long time.

Then my friend Tom, a very successful businessman, stopped over one day and started telling me about how many times he had been treated unfairly. At one point, he said he was on the brink of losing everything and he was questioning God about how unfair it was. After he stewed in anger and bitterness for a long while, he said he finally realized he just needed to trust God and surrender the business to Him. He said he struggled for another six months but decided he needed to trust God. All of a sudden the guy that took his business and market share suddenly closed his business, and all that he took from Tom plus all of the other additional business he had obtained was given back to Tom. It was the first time Tom's business actually made a profit, and the rest is history.

> *For God did not give us a spirit of timidity or cowardice*
> *or fear, but [He has given us a spirit] of power and of love*
> *and of sound judgment and personal discipline [abilities*
> *that result in a calm, well-balanced mind and self-control].*
> (2 Timothy 1:7 AMP)

The choice we have is clear. We can choose to blame others for why we aren't prospering or we can choose to be blessed, but we can't have both. We can put our trust in God, begin to work the principles we have learned in the proverbs, and expect great things to happen in our future. If we have any doubts, then we realize it is the devil talking lies, so we just refuse to listen. When we learn to master our emotions, we can then control our destiny!

God does not give us a spirit of fear. We must learn to discern God's truth from the enemy's lies.

The solution to any situation is to let it go, give it to God. We need to surrender the pain, the unfair situation, and the emotional distress to Him, and then replace those negative thoughts with positive ones.

In Dr. Wayne Dyer's book *Wishes Fulfilled*, he writes, "It is your decision to change that creates the possibility of change within you. Whenever you're experiencing discomfort or sadness, rather than trying to change the thought behind your emotional state, instead just put it back onto the never-ending conveyor belt of thoughts and then select a different thought. Keep doing this until you've selected a thought that allows you to feel good and you're no longer condemning yourself for creating unhappy thoughts."

Every time that hurt comes up and tries to affect us negatively, we just choose a new thought and entertain that one instead of the negative one.

Notice the word "try"—it implies failure. If I said, "I will try to trust God," it means that I really don't. If I say, "I will trust God," it means that I will. It's time to let go of the effort to change and just choose to change. Al Pacino said it best: "We can stay here and get the crap kicked out of us or we can fight our way back into the light. We can climb out of hell one inch at a time. Now what are you going to do?" Maybe it's time we let go of our stories that justify our current or past circumstances that may have put us in a negative place, and realize that where we are now is not the end of the story. I think bitterness can take root in the time between when we surrender and the time we are waiting for God's victory. Maybe God wants us to change before he changes our circumstances.

The $100 Bill Test

Holding a crisp new $100 bill in my hand, I asked my audience if any of them wanted it. Of course, everyone raised their hand. Then I crumpled that $100 bill into a ball and stomped on it and asked if anyone still would want it. Everyone raised their hand. Then I asked them if I ran over it with my car, spit on it, and threw dirt on it, who would want the $100 bill. Everyone raised their hand and said they would still take it. Why? It was because the $100 did not lose its value even though it experienced all those "negative" things. You and I are just like that $100 bill. Sometimes life stomps on us, spits on us, and throws dirt on us, but the good news is that we never, ever lose our value as far as God is concerned. God does not play favorites, either. We must learn to see our value from God's point of view. We are made in God's image, and God never makes a mistake. Likewise, when we receive leads, and maybe they are buried or never used, we might perceive them as having less value. The truth is, leads "business cards" don't expire.

> *For You formed my inward parts; You wove me in my mother's womb. I will give thanks to You, for I am fearfully and wonderfully made; Wonderful are Your works, and my soul knows it very well.* (Psalm 139:13-14)

"Sacrifice what you are for what you can become. If people can't do something themselves, they're going to tell you that you can't do that. You want something, go get it. Period!" – *Will Smith*

Pro-Verb Action Steps:

> *The thoughts and purposes of the [consistently] righteous are honest and reliable, but the counsels and designs of the wicked are treacherous.* (Proverbs 12:5 AMP)

Go back over the seven deadly sins of sales, define them, and honestly answer the questions under each one. Especially notice where your thought patterns may need to be realigned. The victory over the seven deadly sins of sales begins with changing your thoughts and purposes.

1. Pride: As a Sales Sin, this refers to putting others _____ and talking _____ about the competition.
> *Have I found that I sometimes think I am better than my competition?*
> *Do I put them or their product down trying to make me and my product look superior?*
> *Have I spread gossip about others because I am insecure about myself?*
> *What do I need to do to change this destructive thought pattern?*

2. Greed: As a Sales Sin, this refers to taking on _____ or _____.
> *Have I stolen a referral that was not really mine?*
> *Have I tried to sell a product to a customer that I know they did not need just to make a sale?*
> *What do I need to do to change this destructive thought pattern?*

3. Wrath: As a Sales Sin, this refers to losing your _____.

Do I sometimes get so angry I want to "fire" my customer?

Do I ever use sarcasm to cover up my anger?

Have I tried to justify my anger?

What destructive behavior have I seen in my life as a result of this unresolved anger?

What do I need to do to change this destructive thought pattern?

4. Slothfulness: As a Sales Sin, this refers to _____ others for our own _____ of results.

Have I found myself blaming others when I do not achieve the results I desire?

Have I found myself not following through on my commitments?

What do I need to do to change this destructive thought pattern?

5. Envy: As a Sales Sin, this refers to being _____ of someone else's_____.

Do I find myself comparing myself to others?

Do I sometimes feel I am smarter or better than a colleague who landed a big account?

Have I felt that they do not deserve what they have received?

What do I need to do to change this destructive thought pattern?

6. Gluttony: As a Sales Sin, this refers to being a _____.

Do I overcompensate for not wanting to face certain issues in my life by working too much?

What do I need to do to change this destructive thought pattern?

7. Lust: As a Sales Sin, this refers to focusing on your _____ over your customers' _____.

What do I crave more than God?

Do I seek fame and power or to exert dominance over someone?

Do I focus more on my own needs or what is best for my customer?

What do I need to do to change this destructive thought pattern?

Wisdom from the Pro-Verbs

▸ *Real motivation is having a goal to fulfill that is outside of oneself.*

▸ *If you embrace your place and count the blessings that you do have, those blessings will start to multiply.*

▸ *The solution to your situation is to let it go, give it to God.*

▸ *God does not give us a spirit of fear.*

▸ *You must learn to discern God's truth from the enemy's lies.*

▸ *Every time that hurt comes up and affects you negatively, just choose a new thought and entertain a positive one instead of the negative one.*

This list in Philippians 4:8 will help you realign and begin to change any negative thoughts to consistently honest and positive thoughts so you can effectively counteract the seven deadly sins of sales.

> *Finally, believers, whatever is true, whatever is honorable and worthy of respect, whatever is right and confirmed by God's word, whatever is pure and wholesome, whatever is lovely and brings peace, whatever is admirable and of good repute; if there is any excellence, if there is anything worthy of praise, **think continually on these things [center your mind on them, and implant them in your heart].*** (AMP emphasis added)

CHAPTER 2

Earning a Doctorate in Selling

Where there is no guidance, the people fall, but in the abundance of counselors there is victory. (Proverbs 11:14)

W hen I think of someone who has earned their doctorate, I know they have worked extraordinarily hard to be considered the "best of the best" because it is the highest honor they can achieve in their field of study. These are people we seek to model ourselves after when we set our goals no matter what our chosen career.

In sales we don't receive a diploma that says we have worked really hard and earned that Ph.D. after our name, but we do get a big paycheck that proves we have put our time in and done things with a spirit of excellence. If I want to know how to achieve success in sales, I am going to seek out someone who cannot only talk the talk, but has a proven track record of success.

When I think of a doctor of medicine, I think of someone who has pushed their way through the rugged terrain of chemistry and biology to become an expert in their field of study. That is why when we have a medical problem, we go to a medical doctor with a degree in his field of study.

We can pull from these two kinds of "doctors" to construct our methodology for success and earn our doctorate in selling. For example, when we go to see a medical doctor seeking an answer to a specific issue in our lives, they will first conduct an *examination* and ask *questions* to determine the cause of the problem. Second, they will do a *diagnosis* based on their expertise, and then they will give us a *prescription* to specifically deal with these issues.

Many of us are successful in some areas of our lives and yet we struggle in other areas. We may be able to self-diagnose a problem, but find it challenging to find a prescription or solution. Many times it's because we haven't taken the time to "master" our craft and earn our doctorate in selling. We need to combine all these methodologies and develop our own personal formula for success.

The Formula for Success

▸ **Decide** what you want (know your outcome, be specific).
▸ **Determine why** you want it (which creates inner motivation and commitment).
▸ **Measure what** you're getting (methodically measure the results).
▸ **Change** your approach until you get your desired outcome.

> **A real goal is based on a conscious decision**
> **that cuts off all other possibilities except**
> **what we've committed to do.**

The first step is to **decide** what it is you really want and set a specific goal. If you have set this same goal year after year, then you are simply stating a preference. In other words, if you are saying, "I'd **like to be** thinner, richer, happier, etc.," you are probably not actually doing anything to achieve it.

A real goal is based on intelligent, massive actions, not "I hope this works." Be specific with your goals. You must stop "wishing" and "hoping" and saying "I know I should" and make a sincere decision for change that you are willing to put into action.

In order to make a real decision for change, you must **determine why you want** to attain this goal so you can cut off any other possibility than the one you've decided you want. Only then will you fully make the commitment to change. Commitment means to be emotionally compelled and obligated to do what you say you are going to do.[8] If you are not fully committed to a massive action plan of change, you will fall short of your goal. If you say you are going to do something then don't follow through, you are practicing failure and will lose trust in yourself and the trust of your clients as well.

It's not where you are starting that matters, it's where you're determined to end up that makes the difference!

The key is to **measure what you're getting**, which takes from two days to two weeks after taking action. You must be able to methodically measure the results of your massive action plan of change to determine if your approach is working and if you are truly making progress.

Change is inevitable; progress is not.

---

[8] © 2015 *Merriam-Webster*, Incorporated

The key to **effective progressive change** is flexibility in your approach. The more flexible you are, the more successful you will be. Salespeople tend to sell to people that are "like" them. However, the most successful salespeople can mold themselves and become more flexible in their approach to get a new outcome as needed.

Setting Achievable Goals

You cannot hit a target that you cannot see.

Goal setting is the process of deciding what you want to accomplish and devising a plan to achieve the result you desire. Goal setting is a two-part process. Effective goal setting means you need to do more than just **decide** what you want to do. You also have to **work** at accomplishing whatever goal you have set for yourself. You have to be proactive.

Goals without action plans are just words or dreams.

For many people, it's the second part of the goal setting definition that's problematic. They know what they want to do, but have trouble creating a plan to get there. Sometimes it is because they have too many goals. If you have fifteen goals, you will get confused and lose focus, so pick two goals—one professional and one personal.

Create a Life, Not Just a Living

It's true that a majority of the people around us spend more time planning a two-week vacation than they do planning their lives. However, that does not make sense if we are trying to achieve measurable goals. We should have a clear, specific vision of the destination to be reached and the dangers to be avoided. Otherwise, we simply drift and accept our circumstances as our only reality. Goal setting is powerful because it directs our focus.

A good analogy is comparing a goal to a magnifying glass. If you focus the magnifying glass against the sunlight at just the right angle and let the rays focus on one spot, the effect will become immediately apparent. However, if the magnifying glass is moved about and the rays directed from one place to another, it has no real power.

In the same way, what you focus on will direct your thoughts and what you meditate on long enough will come out of your mouth. Then what you speak over and over will form your behaviors and thus make up your beliefs. This is why it is so important to set goals with a specific purpose in mind so everything you think about, meditate on, and speak about will be focused on achieving your true goal.

Below is a list of questions I'd like you to answer. "Ahead to 80" is a process to write out what you want to have when you are eighty years old. It helps direct your mind with ideas of what you would like your life to be like. Always state what you want without limitations. If you would like to retire with 1 million dollars, then don't write or think "It's only possible to really have $500,000 because of my current circumstances." The biggest problem with goal setting is that the majority of people just do not think big enough and unintentionally limit their own potential.

AHEAD TO 80

Where do I live? _____

Who am I with? _____

What have my children become? _____

What am I doing? _____

What do I want? _____

How do I feel? _____

Now identify what intentions you have:

Physical Intentions (Be at 15 percent body fat vs. I want to lose weight)

Income Intentions (50K in the bank by December 31)

Business Intentions (Write a book)

Spiritual Intentions (Read the entire Bible)

Community Service Intentions (Volunteer at the homeless shelter two times a month)

Travel Intentions (Go surfing in Costa Rica)

Personal Growth Intentions (Go to a Tony Robbins Seminar and read three books)

Creative Expression Intentions (Design coffee mugs)

Cultural Development Intentions (Learn Spanish)

By listing out what your intentions are, you can get excited about your future. This list can be as long as you like so you get a future worth living for! Writing crystallizes your thinking and forces you to get clear on what you want. When you are clear on your life vision, you can write down measurable goals. This allows you to achieve the steps of success and ultimately success itself.

It's important to have two clear set goals that you can track, and you can also have twenty or more intentions. Perhaps an intention can come to pass by accomplishing one of your goals. If you set out to make an extra $20,000, perhaps that fulfills one of your travel intentions for a beach trip. One really cool idea is to take all of your intentions and create a vision board.

As an example, one of my intentions is to go to the opera in Paris. So, I bought a picture of a gorgeous red gown that says Paris at the bottom. Now every time I walk up the stairs, I see that dress and I think of how I will look and feel in that dress and going to the opera in Paris.

Imagine every picture and knickknack in your home having meaning, reminding you of what you want, and creating that internal excitement for what is to come in your future. This process is great for families as well. Having an entire family sit down and create a future as a family to support one another with their dreams and ambitions is exciting.

> *Bind them continually upon your heart (in your **thoughts**), and tie them around your neck.* (Proverbs 6:21 AMP emphasis added)

This brings up an often-overlooked element that can influence your success: your environment. Everything that we as humans lay our eyes on or listen to generates an equivalent image or sound in our brains. We are usually not aware of these pictures because, if we were, our conscious mind would be constantly overloaded. For example, we may have a beautiful painting hanging in our living room. Our eyes may pass over that painting thousands of times a day. With each time our eyes pass over that painting, at an unconscious level, our brain is matching the image to its equivalent picture stored in our brain. Our mind, based on the law of attraction, is using its creative powers to manifest each of those pictures into our reality.

Some of these images may reflect your dreams, but many could be in contrast to your dreams. Your environment may be preventing your mind from manifesting your goals, so make sure everything in your environment that you can control is positive and focusing you in the right direction. Make your house and your office your vision board. Only have around you that which you like and makes you smile. If you have a lamp you hate, then get rid of it. If you hate the paint color in one of your rooms, change it. Your environment will either inspire you or depress you.

The Bible teaches us in Philippians 4:8 to focus on "Whatever is true, whatever is honorable, whatever is right, whatever is pure, whatever is lovely, whatever is of good repute, if there is any excellence and if anything worthy of praise, dwell on these things." The law of attraction is simply asking us to do the same thing that the Bible teaches. It is a universal model indicating that energy, and essentially our thoughts, are influential in the reality we experience. The concept is to control our thoughts by concentrating on what we want over what we don't want. In exercising this level of thought control, we can manifest what it is we want.

> The **thoughts** and purposes of the [consistently] righteous are
> just (honest, reliable), but the counsels and schemes of the
> wicked are deceitful. (Proverbs 12:5 AMP emphasis added)

Unfortunately, most of us concentrate more on our problems than our solutions. This keeps the problem in our lives. If someone wants to make more money but is constantly thinking about and talking about how broke they are, they will remain broke. If that person can realize that thought doesn't serve them in a positive way and then choose another thought to dwell on, they have just taken control of their destiny. The best indication of how you are thinking is to get a read on how you actually feel. If you feel bad, then recognize that thought as negative and choose a new thought that will make you feel good.

What must be avoided is something called secondary gain. For example, over 90 percent of women in an abusive relationship will go back to the abuser because she focuses on the good that he does to justify and rationalize remaining in that abusive situation. Until she realizes her personal value and focuses in on the pain he is causing her instead of the secondary gain, she will remain in that unhealthy relationship.

How to Systematize Your Day for Success

Setting a goal to write a book is a big deal. It's easy to feel overwhelmed. Setting the date to turn my book into the publisher was one thing; creating a plan of attack to make sure it's done was another. So, instead of saying I was going to work hard the first week of July, I systemized my writing into three times a week with three-hour blocks. This made me feel successful because I knew I could follow a system to achieve it.

Maybe for you it's blocking out a specific segment of time every day for sales calls. Start with a "Daily Must" and pick one thing to do each day that is a money-producing activity and takes less than ten minutes. Find the "one thing" you need to do every day and do it regardless of what's going on in your day. In that way you can fill your pipeline and make yourself feel successful. Maybe you could send one postcard to a past client one day, call one person from your social network the next day, make one cold-call the third day, and call one existing client on the fourth day asking for a referral. Use the fifth day to call any referrals you receive.

It's all about controlling your energy.

You want to fill your pipeline, and if you get in the "habit" of making one referral call or reaching out to one new person a day, that's twenty new people a month. The majority of salespeople only react to who contacts them rather than actually reaching out. That means they are not in control of how they exert their energy. It's better to call one person a day every day than to attempt to make ten, twenty, or fifty calls Friday. You might get sick on Friday or something will come up and then you will feel like a victim of your circumstances. Your emotions will gain control and tell you how you wasted your energy all week and gained nothing. That is when it becomes easy to blame your boss, your company location, your marketing department, etc. for your lack of results.

The truth is, your choices dictate your actions, so if you allow your emotions to dictate your choices, you will feel like a failure or victim. I have given you an exercise to do in the interactive section at the end of this chapter to get you started systemizing your day for success in areas we all have to deal with in our daily lives. It will help you in this area of gaining control of your energy so your emotions do not dictate your choices.

Choose Wisely

> *He who walks with wise men will be wise, but the companion of fools will suffer harm.* (Proverbs 13:20)

Who do you spend time with? Is it the doctors and the experts in the field you want to be successful in or people who are struggling? You choose your friends, whether consciously or unconsciously. Those you choose to surround yourself with will lift you up, keep you stagnant, or bring you down. You are who you associate with. If you are all about earning your Ph.D. in sales, choose to associate with those who will lift you up and motivate you to move forward toward your goals. I have provided a format for interviewing those who emulate success in reaching the same goals you have listed in **Appendix 1: My Model of Success Sample Interview Questions.**

Getting momentum is what it's all about. Momentum is energy! Your thoughts, actions, and surroundings emit a vibrational frequency that can help or hurt you. This is why you want to surround yourself with people that are successful and happy. Just being around them will elevate your vibrational energy. If you need to get out of your office because of the negativity there, then go work in the lobby of a five star hotel for a few hours. The energy there is vibrant! Make sure you are making wise choices concerning who and what you surround yourself with.

> *The lips of the godly speak helpful words, but the mouth of the wicked speaks perverse words.* (Proverbs 10:32)

Whatever thoughts one thinks control how they feel. If one person feels positive emotions and another is feeling negative emotions, whichever one dominates will direct each one's behavior and form their beliefs. All of that equals the outcome for their experience. So, if you are in an "okay" mood and run into someone on the street that is in a "bad" mood, the person with the stronger, more dominant emotion will affect the other person. That person's energy, whether positive or negative, will affect your energy, and this is how people become victims and feel as if they have no control over their lives.

It's better to choose a destination and then change your mind rather than just seeing where life takes you. Yes, there will be detours that you did not plan for and challenges that you didn't anticipate. Can you stay on course despite the objections that life throws at you? A lot will depend on the choices you make on a daily basis. Begin taking control of what you can.

Will you choose the cookie or the gym, the cold-call list or the break room? Every day you will have choices—choose wisely!

Why not be the very best at what you do? There is no room for mediocre results or just getting by. Time to earn your doctorate in selling!

Note: Many of the principles presented in this chapter also apply to building your own business and motivating your employees. I have included a section at the end of the book to help those of you who desire to improve and grow your business. See **Appendix 2: What Makes a Company Great?**

Wisdom from the Pro-Verbs

▸ A real goal is based on a conscious decision that cuts off all other possibilities except what you've committed to do.

▸ It's not where you are starting that matters, it's where you're determined to end up that makes the difference!

▸ Change is inevitable, progress is not.

▸ You cannot hit a target that you cannot see.

▸ Goals without action plans are just words or dreams.

▸ It's about controlling your energy.

▸ Why not be the very best at what you do? There is no room for mediocre results or just getting by. Time to earn your doctorate in selling!

Ask Yourself...

What is the one thing I can do every morning each day of the week toward reaching my goal no matter what my circumstances?

Who do I spend my time with? Is it the doctors and the experts in my chosen field or people who struggle?

Am I choosing wisely when it comes to the things I can control?

Pro-Verb Action Steps:

#1 Decide what you want and why you want it! Set two goals.

#2 Find a model of success and find out what they have done to be successful.[9]

#3 Write out your plan and put action steps into your daily calendar.

#4 Review your results after the first two weeks.

#5 Change your approach if it is not working.

#6 Do your "daily must" action every day no matter what!

Goals without action plans are just words or dreams.

Wheel of Life Chart

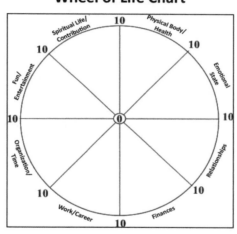

When you look at the Wheel of Life Chart, you will see the different areas we all have in our lives. On a scale from 0 (meaning everything needs work) and 10 (where there is no room for improvement) rate yourself in each area.

---

[9] See **Appendix 1: My Model of Success Sample Interview Questions**

Emotional Wheel of Fitness

Now, for each category, if you are a 6 or below, circle the couch potato. For every area that is 7 or above, circle the trained German Shepherd. This wheel can help you pick two goals to focus on and find a model of success. You can also look at each area and decide what you can systematize.

Choose Wisely

▸ Make a list of the top seven people you spend your time with.

▸ Put a + sign next to the people that challenge you to be a better version of yourself.

▸ Put a – sign next to the people that drain your energy.

▸ Put an = sign next to the people that don't seem to affect you one way or the other.

▸ Now, replace all the – and = with positive people.

CHAPTER 3

Discipline Is the Key to Freedom

*Every prudent and self-**disciplined** man acts with knowledge, but a [closed-minded] fool [who refuses to learn] displays his foolishness [for all to see].* (Proverbs 13:16 AMP)

What separates the successful people from everybody else? Could it be due to their routine physical, emotional, intellectual, and spiritual behaviors and lifestyle choices? What formed these lifestyle choices in the first place? What motivates a person to a disciplined life?

If you are physically fit, you probably have a routine or lifestyle of working out and eating well. Emotionally healthy people rarely explode into fits of anger or bouts with depression because they have discovered effective ways of dealing with the emotional ups and downs of life. Those who are growing intellectually are generally avid readers and spend time intentionally seeking wisdom. Spiritually strong individuals use their faith to sustain them during trials and tribulations and consistently stay connected with those who are like-minded.

*Now every athlete who [goes into training and] competes in the games is **disciplined** and **exercises self-control in all things**. They do it to win a crown that withers, but we [do it to receive] an imperishable [crown that cannot wither].* (1 Corinthians 9:25 AMP emphasis added)

The "world" tells us to do what makes us feel good. TV commercials encourage us to look for things to make us happy. Learning institutions tell us the way to success is through higher education. Life itself offers us many learning experiences, but if experiences alone brought wisdom and fulfillment, then elderly people would all be happy, enlightened masters. If gathering intellectual information from books, magazines, and having various degrees validated us, why aren't the intellectuals totally fulfilled and never depressed?

I see teenagers doing all the things the world says will make them happy—drinking, overeating, over-spending, and indulging in promiscuous behaviors—but with a suicide rate that is 5,000 times higher today than it was ten years ago. They are doing the things that can bring pleasure and instant gratification, yet they are obviously not truly fulfilled in one or more of these four areas. Why do some people choose abstinence and wait to indulge in that pleasure until married, while others act on it when they feel like it? What motivates a person to eat fruits and vegetables rather than fries and cake? Why do some hide under the covers when adversity hits while others triumph over their circumstances?

*Be sober [**well balanced and self-disciplined**], be alert and cautious at all times. That enemy of yours, the devil, prowls around like a roaring lion [fiercely hungry], seeking someone to devour.* (1 Peter 5:8 AMP)

Why do some choose a well-balanced and self-disciplined life? Some would argue it is due to their "upbringing," but that excludes those that rose above their circumstances. I would argue that it is one's commitment level. True commitment is driven by an understanding of one's purpose. Without purpose, we make decisions based on what is in front of us—if it looks good, I'll eat it! If one's purpose is bigger than the instant gratification of the doughnut, one will refrain from the instant gratification and stay true to their commitment to reach their goal. Commitment means to be emotionally compelled and obligated to do what you say you are going to do. How can you be committed to a purpose that you don't know or don't love?

> *And do not be conformed to this world [any longer with its superficial values and customs], but be transformed and progressively changed [as you mature spiritually] by the renewing of your mind [focusing on godly values and ethical attitudes], so that you may prove [for yourselves] what the will of God is, that which is good and acceptable and perfect [**in His plan and purpose for you**]. (Romans 12:2 AMP)*

The Drive of Purpose

The issue is not the process, it's the drive of purpose that is lacking. People battle themselves all day long when they can't figure out why they can't commit to ten calls a day. They find themselves practicing failure with themselves over and over again when the real issue isn't their lack of commitment, it's their lack of purpose. If they had a strong enough purpose then their commitment wouldn't be in question.

I did an experiment years ago. I took a mediocre salesperson to an orphanage and said, "If you don't make $10,000 this month then these kids won't eat because you are going to foot the bill for this month to care for these children." Guess what? He made $20k.

In order to love what you do, you must do what you love, and if you don't love selling "ink" because it's the only job you have, then find something inside of yourself to use the ink sales for a greater purpose. If you don't, you will lack the discipline needed for true commitment and will feel trapped by trying to do something you do not love doing. Find a purpose that is based on what you desire to become and set a goal to achieve it. If you feel trapped and find you are not fully committed to do what is necessary to fulfill that goal, then it simply is not the right purpose or goal.

> **The key to freedom is discipline, and discipline is the fruit of purpose.**

Accountability: You Can't Manage What You Don't Measure

Discipline weighs ounces, while regret ways tons. – Jim Rohn

Once we have defined our purpose and set our goals, we are ready to be crafted into the best version of ourselves. Years ago, I took a stone carving class and the instructor told me to envision my end result and to chip away at anything that did not fit that vision. We must first see who we want to become. Then we must chip away at any negative habit that results in us feeling bad about ourselves or doing the opposite of what we truly want to achieve. We must bend and twist ourselves like clay into that vision of our purpose. The best way to start is to create new empowering habits.

Have you heard that when someone stops smoking they end up replacing cigarettes with food? We have to anticipate the hardships that rear their ugly heads and prepare for them ahead of time. That means disciplining ourselves to work out and having a glass of water anytime we have a craving that presents itself when we are changing.

> **The key to discipline is wanting your goal more than the temporary pleasure.**

If you have your purpose and have set a goal but notice within the first two weeks that you are not doing what is necessary to get to that goal, then you need leverage. You must put yourself in an environment where you are empowered to change. "Burn the boats to get the island" simply means you have to put yourself in a position where the only option is to succeed. You must only focus on getting results. To do this you may need a coach as an accountability partner.

> **The key is intentionally putting yourself in environments that supports what you want.**

Accountability keeps us in alignment with what we say we want. Success comes when what we think, speak, and do are all in alignment with our purpose. A coach keeps us in check for what our purpose is when the enemy rears its ugly head. We need to choose an accountability partner that is more disciplined than we are because we are who we spend time with, just like we are what we eat.

In his book *Rhythm of Life*, Matthew Kelly says that our legitimate needs fall into four categories: physical, emotional, intellectual, and spiritual. He says, "A tree with strong roots grows strong. A tree with strong roots bears much fruit. A tree with strong roots bears good fruit. A tree with strong roots can weather any storm. If a tree is uprooted and replanted often, it will not be able to sink its roots deep into the earth, and therefore will not grow strong or be fruitful." All of this is true not only for a tree, but also for a person.

> **Discipline is the key to developing strong physical, emotional, intellectual, and spiritual roots.**

Discipline is about building a trusting relationship with yourself. Just be consistent and deliberate, then repeat. If you say you are going to go to the gym at 5 p.m. today but don't do it, you are practicing failure with yourself. Achieving your goals is about self-control. If you don't feel like doing something, you probably won't, unless you discipline yourself.

Here are some key ideas to enhance self-discipline:

▸ Get clear on your outcome by setting your focus.

▸ Create a system to follow and create new rituals.

▸ Set aside scheduled blocks of time to achieve specific goals. Control your time with your choices, not with your feelings.

▸ Get an accountability partner and set yourself up for success.

Getting Organized

The cause of many frustrations in moving toward this more disciplined life is simply due to a lack of systems or processes. Remember, you can't control the pitch, but you can control your swing! Without a vision or plan you are winging it. If you are winging it, distractions will monopolize your time. To get a handle on distractions, you need to understand the differences between your tasks list, your to do list, and your appointments.

Tasks List: Specific projects that have deadlines.

To Do List: Things that need to get done with no specific timeline.

Appointments: Meetings with another person or meetings with yourself to complete high priority tasks.

To begin to **weed out the distractions**, answer these questions with a simple yes or no.

Do you have more than ten business cards on your desk right now? _____

Do you have more than fifty emails in your inbox? _____

Do you rely on post-it notes, notepads, baggies of business cards to follow up? _____

Do you wake up in the middle of the night thinking about someone you need to call? _____

Have you ever told a client you would call at a certain time but then forgot? _____

Is your Outlook/Gmail/CRM a data dump? _____

Do you know how to find who you are looking for? _____

Systems run your business and people run those systems. However, we are people of emotion, and unless we set up a system that is logical we will let our emotions rule over us. The average salesperson has 7-17 systems. However, if you have numerous systems, you will drop the ball. You must discipline yourself to get organized and get it down to:

One place where you house your contacts.

One place to put notes on each prospect.

One place to write daily tasks and to do's.

One place where you put all of your appointments. You **cannot** have a paper calendar, an outlook calendar, a phone calendar, and a personal calendar.

Here are some fundamentals to get you started:

- Manage contacts from "one" place – make sure you link referrals.
- Do what is hardest first! That's right, make the cold-call.
- Create policies for your time. Macy's has a 30-day return policy. Coupons have expiration dates. What is your policy for your time?
- Cleaning does NOT equal organizing.
- Stop doing laundry in the middle of the day. Do the important tasks that create value in the middle of the day.
- Work with your energy cycles.
- Language shapes your emotion (nutritious vs. delicious). Whichever word you say, the choice will determine what kind of food you eat! Will it be a nutritious snack or a delicious snack? You decide.
- Revisit your goals and make sure you are following the Success Formula.

Success Formula:
1. Know your outcome (clarity is power).
2. Know why it's a must (purpose = power).
3. Know what you are getting (evaluate in the first two weeks).
4. Change your approach **until** you get your outcome! (persevere)

I've always had an all or nothing mentality, so when I decided I was going to paint the garage, I was going to paint the entire garage. However, what I found was that I had underestimated what it would take and when I couldn't complete it on that day, I felt like I had failed. I allowed this to distract me from completing my goal. I can't tell you how many times I wanted to clean the entire kitchen, but got distracted and found myself not committing to my word because I was overwhelmed by the size of the project.

Discipline requires perseverance.

*And endurance (fortitude) develops maturity of character
(approved faith and tried integrity). And character [of
this sort] produces [the habit of joyful and confident hope...*
(Romans 5:4 AMP)

Here is the solution I came up with to discipline myself to clean my
kitchen. I started with fifteen minutes and cleaned out one drawer. By
tackling this big job in small increments of time, I felt successful and was
able to complete it.

It's all about controlling our energy and making progress. The secret
to happiness is progress. We have to move forward through discipline and
perseverance. Do not focus on the large task. Break it down into man-
ageable parts. Complete just one part, and we will feel good. Then we are
ready to begin working on the next part and so on until the big job is done.

The Discipline of Pruning

*Any branch in Me that does not bear fruit [that stops bearing]
He cuts away (trims off, takes away); and He cleanses and
repeatedly prunes every branch that continues to bear fruit,
to make it bear more and richer and more excellent fruit.*
(John 15:2 AMP emphasis added)

A deeper issue that we must address is the process of pruning. God
is the vine and we are the branches and God will cut back or prune any
branch that doesn't continually bear fruit. Consider this book a pruning
process. We must cut off that which is dead and not working and allow

new life to grow. This is a tough area of discipline because we tend to become comfortable in the way we are doing things. However, inspiration and enthusiasm have a way of breaking us free from our current circumstances so we can once again experience growth.

When we do not feed our enthusiasm with new inspiration, we may become trapped in a rut and stifle new growth. The word "enthusiasm" means strong excitement, passion, and zeal.[10] One of the ways I have found to counteract a lack of enthusiasm is to prune my negativity with thankfulness for what I have already accomplished.

If we can't get ourselves out of the negative energies that want to trap us into thinking that we can't accomplish our goals or follow our schedules, we need to do something that has proven to work. Let's try God's way.

> *In the morning o Lord, you hear my voice; in the morning I lay my request before you and wait in expectation.* (Psalm 5:2-3)

Let's give God our burdens and let him go before us to set our path straight and let us walk in expectation of the good things our hearts desire. Let's fix our gaze on that which can't be seen, the hopes and desires of our hearts, and realize God desires we accomplish all that he has designed us to be and will supply us with what we need.

> *And the God of all grace. Who bestows all grace. Who hath called us unto his eternal glory. After that ye have suffered a while. You may be called to suffer for a season, but it will soon be over. Make you perfect. He will supply every need, leave nothing wanting.* (1 Peter 5:10 KJV)

---

[10] © 2015 *Merriam-Webster*, Incorporated

Become a Master of Discipline and Execute Your Plan

> *"If you do not know what you want from life, every-thing will appear either as an obstacle or a burden."*
> – Matthew Kelly

The majority of people live their lives by default. Do you want to decide where and when you make progress or just let others decide for you? It is your choice.

> *"Shall we have a vision of the destination to be reached, the dangers to be avoided, or shall we simply drift?"*
> – Charles Hannel

Anything worth having will require hard work. If you want a nicely manicured lawn, a strong and trustworthy relationship, or a well-written article, you must nurture and cultivate it. You must discipline yourself to focus on what is important to you in order to develop it into something of value and worth.

> *So prepare your minds for action, be completely sober [in spirit—steadfast, **self-disciplined**, spiritually and morally alert].* (1 Peter 1:13 AMP emphasis added)

If you lived in a million-dollar home, would you do whatever necessary to protect it? You would probably install a security system. However, unless you arm that security system while you are away, it is useless in protecting your million-dollar investment. You are that million-dollar investment. You are a valuable resource with an installed security system of sales tools in hand. However, you need to be sure you know how to "arm" your systems.

> *Whoever loves discipline loves knowledge, but whoever hates correction is stupid.* (Proverbs 12:1)

Without discipline, growth is impossible.

Discipline involves training yourself rather than trying. When we tell others we will "try" something, what we are doing is leaving room and preparing for failure. When we have been trained and practice the right techniques over and over again, we are prepared to do it well. While the old saying "Practice makes Perfect" isn't always true, the saying "Practice makes Permanent" does hold true. When we consistently practice and train for the skills we desire to hold, they become a permanent part of who we are. The skillset moves from being something we desire to do to being a permanent fixture in our lives.

Building Daily Discipline

These are the proverbs of Solomon, David's son, king of Israel.
*Their purpose is to teach people **wisdom and discipline**,*
to help them understand the insights of the wise.
*Their purpose is to teach people to **live disciplined and successful lives**,*
to help them do what is right, just, and fair.
These proverbs will give insight to the simple,
knowledge and discernment to the young.
Let the wise listen to these proverbs and become even wiser.
Let those with understanding receive guidance
by exploring the meaning in these proverbs and parables,

the words of the wise and their riddles.
(Proverbs 1:1-6 NLT emphasis added)

Practice makes permanent in the area of follow through as well. If you set out to complete a task, but do not follow through to complete that task, then you are essentially practicing failure. The difference between successful people and lazy people is the application of these principles from Proverbs that breed character and in turn bring success, fulfillment, and happiness. Ask yourself what you would do if you knew you couldn't fail. Now go out and do that!

If we were building a home for ourselves, think of how carefully we would plan every detail. We would study every plan, inspect and carefully select every material, and oversee every contractor as they built every aspect of our home. Yet, how careless we are when it comes to building our mental home, which is infinitely more important than any physical home.

Everything that builds our mental home depends upon the character of the materials that we allow to enter into its construction. If we have filled our minds with feelings of fear, worry, anxiety, or doubt, then the materials of our mental home cannot bear the good fruit of discipline and confidence. If we store away only courageous, optimistic, and positive thoughts, we will reap the benefits.

Like a dog that returns to its vomit is a fool who repeats his folly. (Proverbs 26:11)

We need to throw any kind of negative thoughts onto our mental scrap pile and refuse to associate or be identified by our negative thoughts. Then, and only then, will the mental materials that have been used to build our mental homes be of the highest quality. We will reap the rewards of a well-built and sustained inner world.

Perhaps we need to do a little mental housecleaning and some pruning to get rid of that which does not deliver what we seek, so there is ample room to grow.

Letting Go Exercise

Find a comfortable place to sit and remove all tension by completely relaxing. This will take some time, so do not look at your watch. Relax. Then mentally let go of all the adverse emotions such as hatred, anger, worry, jealousy, envy, sorrow, trouble, or disappointment by voluntary intention and persistence. Imagine placing each feeling into a special machine that reconfigures the thought into its opposite and then the machine will release the new thought into your universe. This is a daily activity that has to be repeated. Then grab onto that which you would rather hold onto. Grab onto the positive and optimistic thoughts that you wish to define you. Stop entertaining thoughts that do not serve or empower you. Realize the truth and stop validating that which doesn't serve you.

The reason some people cannot do this consistently is because they allow themselves to be controlled by their emotions instead of by their intellect. Those who will be guided by their intellect will gain the victory. The ultimate truth is that good is stronger than evil. When you feel evil is stronger, that is the time to choose discipline and allow yourself to affirm the good, proving that the good is stronger. Use the **Substitute a Constructive Thought for a Destructive Thought** exercise at the end of the chapter to get you started.

Identifying beliefs that don't serve us and changing them moves us in a positive direction. I had a client tell me once that she thought God was punishing her. One of her colleagues mentioned she felt like God was just challenging her. Perspective is everything!

Remember, a builder cannot build a structure of any kind until they have first received the plans from the architect. The architect must get them from his or her imagination. Know why you are building this structure and then make your plans to achieve it. You are the architect of your life!

A wise man will hear and increase in learning. (Proverbs 1:5)

Wisdom from the Pro-Verbs

▸ The key to discipline is wanting your goal more than the temporary pleasure.

▸ The key is intentionally putting yourself in an environment that supports what you want.

▸ The key to freedom is discipline and discipline is the fruit of purpose.

▸ Discipline is the key to developing strong physical, emotional, intellectual, and spiritual roots.

▸ Systems run your business, not your feelings.

▸ Discipline requires perseverance.

▸ Without Discipline, Growth is Impossible.

Ask Yourself...

What would I do if I knew I couldn't fail? _____

Am I entertaining thoughts that serve and empower me? _____

If not, what do I need to change? _____

Am I creating my life by design or by default? _____

Do I want to decide where and when I make progress or just let others decide for me? _____

Who do I want to become? _____

*What do I need to chip away to achieve it?*_____

What boats do I need to burn to get to my island of success?

_____

Pro-Verb Action Steps:

> *Poverty and shame will come to him who neglects discipline,*
> *but he who regards reproof will be honored.* (Proverbs 13:18)

Here are some key ideas to enhance self-discipline in your life:

▸ Get clear on your outcome by setting your focus.

▸ *What is your purpose, what is your focus?*_____

▸ Create a system to follow.

▸ *What is the first step in your self-discipline system?*_____

▸ Set aside scheduled blocks of time to achieve specific goals.

▸ *What is the goal and when are you going to do it?*_____

▸ Control your time with your choices, not with your feelings.

▸ *Write out a declaration of what you are going to do. Post it where you can see it!*_____

▸ Get an accountability partner and set yourself up for success.

▸ *Who is your accountability partner?*_____

Here are some fundamentals to get you started:

▸ Manage contacts from "one" place – make sure you link referrals.

▸ Do what is hardest first! That's right, make the cold-call.

▸ Create policies for your time. *What is your policy for your time?*_____

▸ Cleaning does NOT equal organizing. *Where will you start organizing?*_____

- What important tasks that create value do you need to do in the middle of the day? _____

- Work with your energy cycles. *When do you have the most energy?*_____

- Language shapes your emotion (nutritious vs. delicious). Whichever word you say, the choice will determine what kind of food you eat! Will it be a nutritious snack or a delicious snack? You decide.

- *Monitor your language for the next 24 hours. What do you need to change?* _____

- Revisit your goals and make sure you are following the Success Formula.

Success Formula:

- Know your outcome (clarity is power). My outcome is _____

- Know why it's a must (purpose = power). My purpose is _____

- Know what you are getting (evaluate in the first two weeks). How am I doing? _____

- Change your approach **until** you get your outcome! (persevere) What do I need to change first? _____

Substitute Constructive Thought for Destructive Thought

A very powerful exercise is called the "Just Cuz" card. I developed this card as a way to intentionally put out good energy and lift people up.

First, identify someone that either you are angry at or someone that was a difficult customer or perhaps someone that you might take for granted.

Write that person's name down on a sheet of paper and then write out 2 or 3 qualities or attributes that you like about this person. (Everyone has good qualities, and it is our responsibility as Christians to draw them out.)

Then, next to each quality or attribute, write out the proof that they have that quality.

The objective is to dig deep and find the personality trait that person has, but might not see it in themselves.

When you send this card to someone that made you angry or did you wrong, this is about improving that relationship. It is not about getting a response. It is about putting out into the world forgiveness and love, and it is about being the bigger person.

I had a gentleman in one of my classes, and when we were doing this exercise he said, "I left my wife and daughter when she was two months old and she is twenty-one now. If I send her this card, she will just want to talk about why I left and it may hurt her even more." I replied, "Send it." So, he did, and now she lives with him in Florida.

I had a man that wrote a "Just Cuz" card to his wife outlining what he loved about her, and she called me after she got the card because she was about to file for divorce but got the "Just Cuz" card.

I had a real estate agent send it to her client after she sold her house, and the client sent her three referrals. Now she sends one "Just Cuz" card a day.

This is an excellent exercise to practice when you might be overburdened with all your own issues of life. The best way to channel negative energy is to make someone else's day.

I wrote out a "Just Cuz" card to my dad, and a year later, at Christmas, he said that was his peak for the year! So, whose day will you impact positively?

Keep a record of these cards and the responses you get in your journal.

A generous person will prosper; whoever refreshes others will be refreshed. (Proverbs 11:25)

CHAPTER 4

The 10 Commandments of Sales

The beginning of wisdom is: Acquire wisdom; and with all your acquiring, get understanding. (Proverbs 4:7)

T he Ten Commandments were given by the creator God to show us how to live a better life and to please God (Exodus 20:1-17).

You shall have no other gods before me.

You shall not make idols.

You shall not take the name of the Lord your God in vain.

Remember the Sabbath day, to keep it holy.

Honor your father and your mother.

You shall not murder.

You shall not commit adultery.

You shall not steal.

You shall not bear false witness against your neighbor.

You shall not covet.

It's important to note that Jesus came to challenge our motives and wants us to turn our hearts towards others. Therefore, as you read through these sales strategies, make sure your heart is right. That means in all business transactions we must be honest and kind.

> *Never let loyalty and kindness leave you! Tie them around your neck as a reminder. Write them deep within your heart.* (Proverbs 3:3)

Let us be transparent, kind, and display integrity as our character is what our clients see first.

> *Anyone can find the dirt in someone. Be the one that finds the gold.* (Proverbs 11:27)

The 7 Undisputable Laws of Selling

Follow-up determines the winner. Perseverance wins.

Discipline determines your destiny. Self-control is controlling yourself.

No means "no perceived value at this time." Patience brings the sale—eventually everyone buys. Don't burn your bridges.

Manage your contacts from one place. Be organized and have one system.

It is always better to beg for forgiveness than ask for permission.

God already defeated the devil, so don't believe his lies. Everyone is designed for success.

The number one killer of results is an attitude of minimalism. Think big!

The 10 Keys to Increasing Sales

1. Don't Love Them and Leave Them

This is number one because we must love or appreciate our clients and never leave them after we complete the sale. That behavior seems to be a contagious disease in sales today. We love our client because they bought from us, but then we leave them, not because we are mean people, mostly because then the customer service department takes over and we move on. In reality, the relationship is with the salesperson and because the salesperson does not stay in contact, that customer will grow cold over time. At that point, the clients don't even remember your name.

Note: The number one reason a prospect or client doesn't call a salesperson is because they don't have or can't find their phone number! The number one reason a salesperson doesn't follow up with a prospect or client is because they can't find their phone number either. You must systematize your sales process. You must have a follow-up strategy! Make it a repeatable process.

> **It costs five times as much to attract a new customer than it does to keep a current one.**

2. Stay Connected because 80 Percent of All Sales Are Made on the Fifth to Twelfth Contact

- 48% of salespeople never follow up with a prospect
- 25% of salespeople make a second contact and stop
- 12% of salespeople only make three contacts and stop

Only 10 percent of Salespeople Make More Than Three Contacts

- ▸ 2% of sales are made on the first contact
- ▸ 3% of sales are made on the second contact
- ▸ 5% of sales are made on the third contact
- ▸ 10% of sales are made on the fourth contact

The key is how you leave a voicemail. A better approach is to realize people are just busy, and you cannot sell **anything** over voicemail. See sales commandment number ten for how to master voicemail.

3. Cherish Referrals Since One Referral Is Equivalent to Fifteen Cold-Calls

Cold-calling and prospecting in general are necessary and very effective when you have a specific method to follow. Start with calling **all** your past customers and follow the referral call strategy discussed in an upcoming chapter. Before you do that, identify and plan for what kind of referral you want. You want a vertical referral, someone that is your ideal client. Create a referral form to help you start tracking your referrals and to carry with you so that you can write down the referrals you are given. You can track referrals in your email system as well by writing down the referee's name and reference both names in the notes section. This way, when you look up a contact, both names will pop up so that you can remember who referred them. You can also categorize each referral into a "Lead-Referral" folder or category so that you can schedule follow-up calls.

All of this can be done in a CRM as well, but make sure you have your system written out so that if and when you change CRM systems, your strategy isn't changed, resulting in lost contacts.

Yes, you have to follow up with referrals as well and make sure not to spill the beans on voicemail. Do **not** say anything like: "Hi _____ my name is _____ and I'm with xyz realty and I got your name and number from _____ and she said that you are looking to buy a home. I would love to help you!" This is a very poor approach because you have put yourself in a situation where you sound like everybody else. At best, you have a 50/50 chance that they will call you back.

Also, notice when you say "I would love to help you" it sounds like you are a beggar. You are the salesperson, of course you would love to help them, but what would they love? You must flip that to "What you would love is _____." You must start thinking and speaking in terms of what your client wants, not what you want.

Tips on Referrals

Please remove from your email "My business is built on your referrals" or "The best compliment you can give me is a referral," and replace it with "Who do you know that might be open to re-evaluating their payroll services?" or "Who do you know that might be open to buying a second home?" The difference is not subtle. It is totally about your customer and not at all about you. It is a call to action and not a plea for help. Remember, referrals are not about you, the salesperson. They are always about your customer and making your customer look good with their friends. Compliment your customer by helping their friends. Classy people can sense desperation, and you don't want someone giving you a charity referral, which is a downgraded referral.

4. Never Talk about the Competition

**You have the power when you are
the one asking the questions.**

My mother always said, "You deserve what you tolerate." If you ask "What made you choose your current vendor," then your prospect will tell you. That is **not** what you want because now they are focused on the competition and giving you lots of reasons why they picked them. It will become virtually impossible to sell them in this manner.

Even if they are complaining about their current vendor, they will unconsciously associate you with their competition, which they don't like, and they will group you together. You have to control your prospect's energy and direct them to the solution. Tell your prospect how it's going to be easy and fun.

Never talk about the competition or clarify an objection that makes you repeat a negative. For example, I was working with some new home sales agents and several prospects had just walked through a model home. The prospects looked at the saleswoman and said, "We hate black appliances."

The salesperson said, "Okay, so you hate black appliances."

What the sales woman should have done in this scenario was say "I hear what you are saying, so which would you prefer white, cream or stainless steel appliances?"

Even if they then say "I hate white," she can say "Wonderful, that leaves us with cream and stainless steel. Of those, which do you prefer?"

We must learn to control a prospect's energy.

If a prospect says they are satisfied with their current vendor and the salesperson asks them why they are satisfied, the prospect will give the salesperson 100,000 reasons why they are satisfied. The salesperson will not sell the prospect one single thing.

5. Let Systems Run Your Business, Not Your Feelings

If you don't have a system to follow and you show up to work each day reacting to what the day throws at you, at best you will live paycheck to paycheck.

Having a system in place keeps us on track when we don't feel like doing something. Why do people get personal trainers? Because they hold them accountable and push them to achieve a result.

"Well, it's Monday," you say. "I know this client is just getting back from a trip so I should call them on Wednesday." You are intentionally postponing a call because "they" had a lot going on and your business is based on your feelings and not the value you bring to your client.

If you have enough value to bring to the table, they will listen to you, but if you are just pitching your product hoping they will buy, you will get blown off! News flash! You are an interruption to anyone that you call, but if you provide enough value to them, they will stay on the call. You must be skilled in your business approach and be concise, clear, and articulate what value your product or service can do for your prospect. Make it easy for them to say "Yes." You never want a prospect to get annoyed with you, because if they do that means you are pitching your product/service and not focusing on their needs and wants.

6. Practice the Law of Reciprocity

> *Persuasion is the process of getting your customers to associate the act of not buying to the feeling of pain.*
> – Tamara Bunte

The law of reciprocity tells us that when we give someone a gift, they then feel obligated to give one back. So, start giving gifts! It will increase the odds that that person will feel more attached to you and you will make them feel important. Make sure your attitude is one of service and giving and not expecting anything in return, but knowing that that person is thinking about you fondly.

When I had my baby boy, I needed a nanny; so I interviewed three candidates. All three were fantastic, qualified, and any one of them would have been a great choice. The candidate I chose did something different than the other two—she brought a little stuffed dinosaur for my baby boy. It showed me that she wanted the job and cared the most, so I hired her.

The little things matter. They show diligence, professionalism, and most importantly, that you care about them. Start incorporating gifts into your business at least once a year! I like to send journals or notepads with my client's name embroidered in gold. Maybe you want to send cookies or a stack of pens with a bow around them. It doesn't matter what it is, just do it.

I really love using *Send Out Cards* because I can customize a card and attach a gift and they send it for me. I can even send campaigns and schedule my yearly or quarterly gifts. My friend Gabe started selling send out cards and we set up the system together. I sent my custom card to a prospect that I had been trying to get in with for over a year. He got my card, we went to lunch, and I closed a $15K training contract. Thanks to Gabe, I have a system now that I love. Try it out![11]

Give more than you take. If you ask for a favor, you are taking from them. Stop doing that! Offer them a gift or an invitation instead. You want people to feel welcome and valued. Your attitude must reflect your heart of giving. Remember, if you ask for a favor, your prospect will want one in return and, instead of trying to build your business, your prospect will turn it around and expect you to buy from them. Avoid the classic trap of "this for that."

> **Always keep in mind that people don't buy "things," they buy "benefits," which are the result of what things will do for them.**

---

[11] Give them a call and give them my name, Tamara Bunte, or go to their website, https://www.Sendoutcards.com/proverbsforselling

7. Get Personal

Resistance in a client is a sign of lack of rapport. There are no resistant clients; there are only inflexible salespeople. We must mold ourselves to see our prospect from their perspective of the world. We must respect their perspective. The most successful salespeople are the most flexible because they change their ways to fit the world of their client. The client will not change, but the effective sales leader does change to meet the needs of their client.

We must get personal because that is the best way to build trust. If I am a realtor and my prospect is interviewing three different companies, I want to increase my odds that I will be picked. To do this I want to ask emotional-based questions like how did you meet your spouse? By asking this question, the prospect is now sharing personal information and trusting me with it. So when it comes down to it, they will pick the person that they "trust" the most.

Trust is when the customer feels that you will do what is in their best interest, not your own. Your odds will increase when they can trust you with their personal information. Remember, people don't care how much you know until they know how much you care!

**Consider every prospect as a new friend.
You are a professional friend finder! That is
how the best sales leaders function—they care!**

---

8. Win the Sale – Overcome Objections in a Classy and Witty Way

How do you win over a prospect that says "I'm working with someone already" or "I'm satisfied" or "Send me some information"? If you can't "win" over your prospect, then they will win you over with their objections.

My sales team seemed to get the objection "We have in-house training." Now, I know that their in-house training isn't that great at delivering results, but they don't know this yet. So I say, "I hear what you are saying, but do you by chance know how many advisors the president has?" They usually say no, and my response is "Clearly not enough," which generates a laugh from the prospect. I am changing their perception of their in-house trainers. I then ask a question like "If I gave one of your salespeople a referral and they called my friend three times and they didn't get a call back, what do you train your salespeople to say on the fourth voicemail?" The response is generally a mumbled "Um, um, um." Then I ask my second and third questions and, like magic, they invite me in for a meeting!

Seven out of ten salespeople never ask for the sale and that is the reason they don't get a sale.

At the same time, 80 percent of salespeople focus on and try to convince unqualified prospects to buy from them. This is why asking questions to qualify your prospect is so effective. If you skip the questioning process and let the prospect control the sale, you set yourself up for failure.

9. Obtain Testimonials

Testimonials bring customers, while advertising and marketing bring awareness.

We must ask for testimonials because we can't expect people to send them to us even though they got such great results from our product. We must lead the sales process and we must ask for a referral before or after they buy, and not a year later. If I say I'm great, I'm bragging, but if my customer says I'm great that is independent proof! It's a great way to get your prospect happy before asking for a referral.

Tips on how to write testimonials:
- ▸ Effective testimonials must be specific, not general. (I made x number of calls and got x amount of business versus I made many calls.)
- ▸ A testimonial should show action and make a call to action. (I used to hesitate to make calls, now I got organized and am efficient. Give them a reason to make a decision now.)
- ▸ A testimonial should overcome an objection. (I thought the price was too high, but I bought anyway and realized it was the best value.)
- ▸ A testimonial should reinforce a claim. (I increased my productivity by x and made x more money by making x calls per week.)
- ▸ A testimonial should claim a happy ending such as ease of use, speed of service, special features, etc.

10. Master Voicemail
Here are three sample voicemails you can use:

Hi _____ it's _____ with _____ 704-247-8333, 704-247-8333. Call me.

Hi _____ it's _____ with _____ Let me give you my cell phone, 704-247-8333. Call me.

Hi _____ it's _____ with _____ 704-247-8333. This is in reference to you. Call me.

All of these voicemails abide by the influence laws of sales. You cannot leave a reason why you are calling on voicemail because then there is no reason for them to call you back. You must practice good sales etiquette.

You cannot sell over voicemail, so use any or all of the above voicemail options. You can give your first name and company name or first name and last name, but no company name. You don't want to have your prospect to be able to look you up in their CRM system. You want to be kind of mysterious and intriguing. You want them to call you back! Email is similar: use your first name in an email subject line and you will get an increase in response rate. Just write it out like you would use in the voicemail: Hi _____ it's _____with _____. This is in regards to you. Call my cell at 704-247-8333. Thanks.

You cannot say "Please just call me back and let me know either way if you are still interested in my product." Why not? Because it will make the prospect feel guilty for not calling you back, and guilty people flee. They run really fast. If you do this, then you have effectively shot yourself in the foot and you end the possibility of this person being a prospect.

Remember that there is no magic formula for closing a deal. The magic is in doing everything else well, then having the confidence to ask for a decision. In the next chapter, I will give you wisdom principles, secrets to selling, and show you how language patterns can either sabotage or save your sale.

"Your measure of success is not about being better than anybody else; it's about being better than you used to be."
– Wayne Dyer

Wisdom from the Pro-Verbs

▸ Let us be transparent, kind, and display integrity as our character is what our clients see first.

▸ It costs five times as much to attract a new customer than it does to keep a current one.

▸ One referral is equivalent to fifteen cold-calls.

- You have the power when you are the one asking the questions.
- If you don't have a system to follow and you show up to work each day reacting to what the day throws at you, at best you will live paycheck to paycheck.
- Seven out of ten salespeople **never** ask for the sale and that is **the reason** they don't get a sale.
- Consider every prospect as a new friend. You are a professional friend finder!
- Give more than you take.
- Always keep in mind that people don't buy "things," they buy "benefits."
- Testimonials bring customers, while advertising and marketing bring awareness.

Ask Yourself...

Am I living from paycheck to paycheck?

Am I truly asking for the sale?

Do I consider every prospect a friend?

Do I sell with the best interest of my client in mind?

Am I transparent and kind and do I display integrity?

Pro-Verb Action Steps:

We cannot manage what we do not measure, so take inventory as to where you believe you are in the list of the top ten areas of sales. Then take what's working and discover new ways to improve.

Skill: Rate Yourself (circle)	Your Score	
1. Setting & Achieving Goals	1-2-3-4-5-6-7-8-9-10	_____
2. Telephone Skills/ Follow-up	1-2-3-4-5-6-7-8-9-10	_____
3. Prospecting	1-2-3-4-5-6-7-8-9-10	_____

4.	Time Management/Productivity	1-2-3-4-5-6-7-8-9-10	_____
5.	State-of-Mind Management	1-2-3-4-5-6-7-8-9-10	_____
6.	Presenting/Influence	1-2-3-4-5-6-7-8-9-10	_____
7.	Overcoming Objections	1-2-3-4-5-6-7-8-9-10	_____
8.	Obtaining Referrals	1-2-3-4-5-6-7-8-9-10	_____
9.	Cross Sell/Up Sell	1-2-3-4-5-6-7-8-9-10	_____
10.	Closing the Sale	1-2-3-4-5-6-7-8-9-10	_____

What is the one skill that if you were excellent at would help you increase your income the most? _____

Remember, there is no magic formula for closing. The magic is in doing everything else well, then having the confidence to ask for a decision.

List the 10 Commandments of Sales and write a one-sentence description of each one. Post this list where you can review it every day.

1._____
2._____
3._____
4._____
5._____
6._____
7._____
8._____
9._____
10._____

It's important to note Jesus came to challenge our motives and wants us to turn our hearts towards others. As you implement these sales strategies, make sure your heart is right. That means all business transactions that you do must be honest and kind.

CHAPTER 5

The Golden Book of Sales Wisdom

*Making your ear attentive to skillful and godly Wisdom
and inclining and directing your heart and mind to understanding [applying all your powers to the quest for it]; Yes, if
you cry out for insight and raise your voice for understanding,
if you seek [Wisdom] as for silver and search for skillful and
godly Wisdom as for hidden treasures, then you will understand the reverent and worshipful fear of the Lord and find
the knowledge of [our omniscient] God. For the Lord gives
skillful and godly Wisdom; from His mouth come knowledge
and understanding.... Then you will understand righteousness, justice, and fair dealing [in every area and relation]; yes,
you will understand every good path. For skillful and godly
Wisdom shall enter into your heart, and knowledge shall
be pleasant to you. Discretion shall watch over you, understanding shall keep you.* (Proverbs 2:2-6, 9-11 AMP)

This chapter is a collection of the golden nuggets of wisdom I have
gleaned from studying the proverbs and applying them to my life.

They will begin to infuse your thinking with powerful ways to change your mindset and get you started on the path to acquiring wisdom and getting understanding so you can put them into practice in your own business. It is a culmination of what we have discussed so far. Use it as a review for this first half of the book. As we progress through the rest of the book, I will give you more and more practical ways to use these golden nuggets to bring about true change in your business relationships.

Wisdom Principles

▸ The hardest sale is raising our children. Everyone is in sales! Who is more influential: you, the parent, or the drug dealer?

▸ To be skillful at anything requires practice of the right activities. On average, you must follow up 8-12 times to get a deal; practice frequently and make it a ritual.

▸ Throw all the standard, common folders and brochures away – only the editor will read them.

▸ No marketing piece should be more than six lines down and six words across; if the prospect can't read it in 10 seconds, they won't read it at all.

▸ Never hire a salesperson who waits for business cards to come in before starting to sell; they are a billboard, not a salesperson.

▸ Master what you fear. Bruce Wayne was afraid of bats and became Batman. You become what you fear unless you master it.

▸ If you want to be viewed as a commodity, then pitch people on voicemail. If you want to be a well-trained sales professional with class, use voicemail to get people to call you back so you can establish value.

- If people don't call you back, it's your responsibility to call them back again and again. Under no circumstances can you make the prospect feel guilty for not calling you back.
- Anytime you get a no show on an appointment or a price objection, it means there is not enough perceived value at this time to show up or to buy.
- The reason for your call is NEVER to follow up to an email, letter, brochure or mailing piece.
- Using the phone to set an appointment is much cheaper than an in-person visit. Be careful not to become a professional visitor.
- Do the hardest thing first. Make the cold-call and make a new friend.
- Questions qualify your buyer, not assumptions.
- Rejection is God's protection – Never compromise who you are for a sale. If you do everything in your power and it still doesn't work out, thank God, move on, and learn how to improve.
- You should be working 10-15 deals for every one that you want. Never put all of your eggs in one basket.
- Never make a cold-call and ask to speak to the owner. You must know the owner's name, or the gate keeper will say, "What's this regarding?" If you tell them "Payroll services," they will say "We are all set."
- Never put the lowest-paid person in front of your most valuable asset, the customer!

The Secrets of Selling –How to Make Even More Money
- Thou shalt position yourself to be invited in for a meeting.
- Thou shalt get personal.
- Thou shalt never use a brochure as a selling tool.
- Thou shalt know questions qualify a buyer, not your assumptions.

▸ Thou shalt know business cards and referrals don't expire or go bad.
▸ Thou shalt be prepared to win over every objection.

Cultivate a Mental Attitude That Will Bring You Peace and Happiness

Happy (blessed, fortunate, enviable) is the man who finds skillful and godly Wisdom, and the man who gets understanding [drawing it forth from God's Word and life's experiences], for the gaining of it is better than the gaining of silver, and the profit of it better than fine gold. (Proverbs 3:13-14 AMP)

▸ Thou shalt never lose your cool.
▸ Thou shalt know a sale isn't a sale until they sign on the dotted line and the money is in the bank.
▸ Thou shalt never succumb to stagnation.
▸ Thou shalt never give up. Never.
▸ Thou shalt never blame anyone but yourself for poor results.
▸ Thou shalt know the customer is always right, even if they're wrong.
▸ Thou shalt control your emotions when under pressure.
▸ Thou shalt be unwavering in your faith.
▸ Thou shalt plant seeds of peace.
▸ Thou shalt build each other up.

Win People to Your Way of Thinking
▸ Thou shalt never put your agenda ahead of your customer's needs.
▸ Thou shalt follow their schedule, not their feelings.
▸ Thou shalt send handwritten letters.
▸ Thou shalt be kind and honest in all business transactions.

- Thou shalt see your value from God's point of view.
- Thou shalt believe you **can** make a sale on every call.
- Thou shalt be motivated by hope and not fear.

Be Classy

- Thou shalt never sell (pitch a product/service) over voicemail.
- Thou shalt never stalk someone (calling without leaving a voicemail).
- Thou shalt never love them and leave them.
- Thou shalt never get angry when someone doesn't buy.
- Thou shalt only ask for referrals when the client is in a peak state.

Wisdom Strategies

> *The beginning of Wisdom is: get Wisdom (skillful and godly Wisdom)! [For skillful and godly Wisdom is the principal thing.] And with all you have gotten, get understanding (discernment, comprehension, and interpretation).* (Proverbs 4:7 AMP)

- Thou shalt obtain the order when the prospect is hungry.
- Thou shalt never become a workaholic.
- Thou shalt obtain testimonials.
- Thou shalt obtain vertical referrals.
- Thou shalt have a follow-up strategy.
- Thou shalt always ask for something from each meeting.
- Thou shalt have faith in your sales system.
- Thou shalt always leave a voicemail without leaving a reason.
- Thou shalt sell or be sold! Someone is always selling someone.

- ▸ Thou shalt take good notes on every client.
- ▸ Thou shalt give gifts.
- ▸ Thou shalt see things from the customer's perspective.

Language Patterns that Sabotage You and Save You

> *A man's [moral] self shall be filled with the fruit of his mouth;*
> *and with the consequence of his **words** he must be satisfied*
> *[whether good or evil].*
> (Proverbs 18:20 AMP emphasis added)

- ▸ Thou shalt never say "I'm not here to sell you anything."
- ▸ Thou shalt never ask "Is it a good time to talk?"
- ▸ Thou shalt never ask for permission to follow up.
- ▸ Thou shalt never thank someone for "taking your call."
- ▸ Thou shalt never talk about the competition (or repeat a negative).
- ▸ Thou shalt never leave a reason why you are calling on voicemail.
- ▸ Thou shalt never say "Let's meet so I can tell you about what I do."
- ▸ Thou shalt never use the words "follow up" or "interested" in any sales call.

> *You are snared with the **words** of your lips, you are*
> *caught by the speech of your mouth.* (Proverbs 6:2 AMP
> emphasis added)

Might and Maybe = We do not like to take orders and resent them when we hear them. Therefore, we can use this language pattern to help us persuade others in a gentler and effective way. When you delete *might* and *maybe* from the sentence, it ends up being a command.

You **might** want to take the trash out …**NOW**

You **might** want to buy this **now.**

Maybe you'll want to go ahead with it when you consider…

Don't = Diffuses the pressure and creates a greater sense of urgency. Our brain cannot process negatives, so our brain really reads this sentence without the "don't."

Don't feel as though you have to buy something today.

Don't feel like you have to decide right now.

I **don't** know this opportunity is going to completely change your life…

Secrets = I shouldn't tell you this, but here I go.

Yes, Yes, Yes, the repetitive Yes pattern = Getting the prospect to respond either verbally or internally, so you create a receptive state of mind in the person you are trying to persuade.

"Wouldn't you agree that (rhetorical question)?"

"If that makes sense, it probably also makes sense that (rhetorical statement), doesn't it?"

"So, maybe you want to just take care of delivery now. Would that probably be best?"

Words to Avoid:

Follow up – Would you say this phrase when calling one of your friends? No!

Try – Implies failure. Either do or do not, but don't try.

Interested – Replace with "Open and Willing." People are open but rarely interested.

Checking in – What are you checking in about?

Touching Base – Delete this phrase! Instead say "The purpose of my call is..."

Love to. Like to. Enjoy to. – Avoid because this is all about you and not about the customer. Replace with "you would love, you would like, I think you would enjoy..."

Is this a good time to talk? – Avoid asking this silly question because the person on the other end of the phone will ask "What is this regarding?" Then you will stumble through your pitch and be perceived as a salesperson. They will usually listen for about 5 seconds, then say they are not interested or call them back, which is an indication you provided a reason for them to stay on the phone with you, just not a good enough one. You **must** provide enough value for them to engage in conversation. Remember, you are an interruption no matter when or who you call. Make it worth their time to stay on the phone.

Power Words

> From the fruit of his **words** a man shall be satisfied with
> good, and the work of a man's hands shall come back to him
> [as a harvest]. (Proverbs 12:14 AMP)

According to Kevin Hogan, in his book "The Psychology of Persuasion," he gives us power words that sell. Add these to your emails, marketing pieces, and scripts and notice the difference. I also added a few more that make a big difference in your client's response to you.

Name	Right	Vital
Please	Powerful	Now
Thank you	Improved	Even more

Because	Discovery	Allow
Trust	Proud	Deserve
Results	Easy	That's right
Value	Proven	I'm wondering if…
Exciting	Health	You probably already know…
Fun	Profit	I don't know if…
Guarantee	New	Sooner or later
Advantage	Truth	You can ____ because
Save	You	You might not have noticed
Benefit	Investment	Can you imagine
Security	Happy	Secret
Comfort	Joy	Might
Free	Money	Maybe
Love	Safety	Yes

As a man thinks in his heart so is he. (Proverbs 23:7 NKJV)

You naturally move toward whatever you focus your attention on. The more you think about something, the stronger it takes hold of you. That's why your words are so important. Repeating "I must stop eating so much" or "I need to stop smoking" is a self-defeating strategy. It keeps you focused on what you don't want. You must learn to say it how you want it. "I am eating healthy fresh fruits and vegetables so I can become a healthier me."

> *The words of a [discreet and wise] man's mouth are like deep waters [plenteous and difficult to fathom], and the fountain of skillful and godly wisdom is like a gushing stream [sparkling, fresh, pure, and life-giving].* (Proverbs 18:4 AMP)

If someone is about to get up and speak in public and says to himself "I don't want to be nervous," he sets himself up to be nervous. He will be focused on and thinking about not being nervous. What he should say to himself is "I know my material and I am confident I can present it in a dynamic and powerful way!"

If you say to someone "I'm not pushy," you are subconsciously telling your prospect that "you are pushy." Instead, tell them what you really want them to know about you: "I am super easy going." Then tell them why that is in their best interest. We must give people confidence in us in the sales process.

Failure is another one of those words we should never use. We often confuse failure with feedback, and the two are not the same. Feedback should tell you what you need to change about your approach.

Also, if you don't like prospecting, then it probably means your approach is wrong. All you have to do is surround yourself with people that enjoy prospecting and allow their positive energy to inspire you. You will start to change your mindset.

There are three main reasons why a salesperson hesitates to pick up the phone:

1. Their overall mindset is wrong. They think they are an interruption. They must be convinced that what they have to sell is of value and will benefit their client.

2. They are not at their peak state. They are thinking "I have to make calls" versus "I get to make calls." Just like an athlete warms up before a game, we must warm up before our day. Do this by reviewing one or more of the pro-verbs we have been discussing and get your mindset focused in the right direction.

3. They are not prepared. They don't know what they are going to say; therefore, they cannot articulate what they have to offer. Preparation comes just before getting lucky.

"The quality of your life is in direct proportion to the amount of influence you have over yourself." – Tamara Bunte

In the next chapter, I will give you specifics for obtaining vertical referrals so you can build even stronger relationships with your clients. It's not a question of can you make more money; the question is, will you choose to do what it takes to step up your game?

Wisdom from the Pro-Verbs

For skillful and godly Wisdom shall enter into your heart, and knowledge shall be pleasant to you. Discretion shall watch over you, understanding shall keep you. (Proverbs 2:10-11 AMP)

Happy (blessed, fortunate, enviable) is the man who finds skillful and godly Wisdom, and the man who gets understanding [drawing it forth from God's Word and life's experiences], for the gaining of it is better than the gaining of silver, and the profit of it better than fine gold. (Proverbs 3:13-14 AMP)

The beginning of Wisdom is: get Wisdom (skillful and godly Wisdom)! [For skillful and godly Wisdom is the principal thing.] And with all you have gotten, get

understanding (discernment, comprehension, and inter-pretation). (Proverbs 4:7 AMP)

A man's [moral] self shall be filled with the fruit of his mouth; and with the consequence of his words he must be satisfied [whether good or evil]. (Proverbs 18:20 AMP)

You are snared with the words of your lips, you are caught by the speech of your mouth. (Proverbs 6:2 AMP)

From the fruit of his words a man shall be satisfied with good, and the work of a man's hands shall come back to him [as a harvest]. (Proverbs 12:14 AMP)

As a man thinks in his heart so is he. (Proverbs 23:7 NKJV)

The words of a [discreet and wise] man's mouth are like deep waters [plenteous and difficult to fathom], and the fountain of skillful and godly Wisdom is like a gushing stream [sparkling, fresh, pure, and life-giving]. (Proverbs 18:4 AMP)

Ask Yourself...

Am I confusing failure with feedback?
Am I willing to do whatever it takes to step up my game?
Am I operating from a place of service?
Am I excited about what I have to offer?

Pro-Verb Action Steps:

What's fascinating about studies on the brain is that the serotonin levels in your brain which control your levels of happiness are what pharmaceutical companies target to alleviate depression. However, it has been proven that showing an act of kindness, being a witness to an act of kindness, or receiving an act of kindness significantly increases levels of serotonin in the brain. So if you wish to see more success in your sales business, all you have to do is raise your serotonin levels through giving to others and it will change your state of mind and your environment. Decide what you will practice today to increase your sales and then do a heart check!

Now, let's move on to the second half of the book, which will give you some very practical ways to ask for referrals, establish your value, earn more business, improve your cold-calling (aka friend finding abilities), and even give you a mindset make-over!

CHAPTER 6

How to Ask for Referrals...
The Classy Way

The wise in heart will be called understanding, and sweetness of speech increase persuasiveness. (Proverbs 16:21)

Cold-Calling is super effective if you know what you are doing! What I can't understand is why so many companies emphasize prospecting, cold-calling, and making new friends when the majority of companies I consult with don't even ask their current clients who are people that love them for referrals. The answer is they just don't know how to do it. Referrals have everything to do with the client and the client's friends.

Have you heard the line "Your referrals are the greatest compliment I could receive?" Or, worse yet, "I build my business on your referrals." This is unprofessional because referrals are **not** about **me, myself, and I**. Referrals are not a compliment to you.

> **Referrals are given because your client believes you will make them look good with their friends or clients.**

Has a client ever said "I'll have them call you?" or they won't give you their friend's phone number? It's because they don't **trust** that you will make them look good. Referrals are about your clients building stronger relationships with their clients. You need to convince them you are just the one to help build that relationship for them.

Asking for introductions is also an unprofessional approach. If I ask you to introduce me to the VP of Sales of the XYZ Corporation, that means I'm hoping that you will actually work for me by overcoming every objection that might come up and answering any question about me and my product that they will ask. I'm hoping that you are good enough to sell for me. Worse, I am putting my paycheck in the hands of someone that may never call me because I never got their phone number.

If sales were that easy, we would all just sit back and wait for the phone to ring. That doesn't happen, so we must go out and get what we want. To do this, we must first of all know what we want.

Sheila Neisler says "I don't want light, I want heat." All the colorful brochures in the world might make your company "light" up, but you won't get "heat," meaning prospects calling you from those marketing pieces. The most effective form of advertising is recommendations from the people you already know. The fact is, 80 percent of what drives buying decisions are referrals because they are based on trust.

> **In order to procure a referral, you must have built trust with your client through an attitude of service.**

A better way to ask for a referral is "Who do you know that's super successful like you and might be open to using this product that has made you so successful?" Notice the lack of **me, myself, and I**. The focus is on the client and how you can help them by helping their friend or client be as successful as they are.

That leads us to the very next problem, which is that most companies don't even know their target market. Who do they really want to be referred to?

If I asked you "Who do you know that needs a coach?" you might refer me to your sick, broke, miserable cousin. However, if I asked you "Who needs a coach and owns a company that is super-successful like you and wants to take their business to the next level," now you are thinking about who you know that is a super-successful business owner! Which referral do you really want?

I will never forget my good friend Mel. She has me come and speak to her networking groups every year. A few years ago, we got a bite to eat after one of these events and she asked about my life, my current clients, etc. At that time, I had a client that was literally the devil's best friend. This client had lots of money, but they were very unethical people and I started to complain.

She asked me a question that changed my whole outlook on asking for referrals: "Who do you **want** to work with?"

I blurted out "Christians! I just want to work with Christian business owners!"

Mel said, "Well, you have to meet Tim."

Then I asked the question that would change my whole method of asking for referrals: "Oh, really? What do you like about him?"

She went on and on about how he was a man of integrity, so genuine, and runs a very successful financial firm in Charlotte. She gave me his phone number, I called him, and the rest is history. I worked with his company to help take their sales to the next level. The point is, *I got what I asked for.*

You need to be specific. You want vertical referrals, meaning you want to be referred to people who can afford to hire you. For example, a traditional way to ask for a referral would be "Who do you know that is looking to buy a home in Charlotte?" A vertical referral would be "Who do you know that's financially savvy like you that might be looking for a second home?" Now this is a much classier way to ask for a vertical referral. It presupposes your client would refer you to someone already rich because you are asking for one that is looking to buy a second home.

When I ask most companies if they have a standard referral form and if they have trained their people to ask every new client for a referral, sadly, the answer to both questions is generally "No." Unfortunately, most salespeople have not been trained to practice good sales etiquette. Not only have they not been trained how to ask for a referral, they are not even encouraged to ask the clients they already have established for referrals.

One of the first things I do is show them how to use a referral form. I have included my standard referral form at the end of this chapter, but I also want to show you how to personalize it to get what they really want.

For example, on my referral form it says: *Who else can we make this happy? Who do you know that is a friend or entrepreneur that owns a business with a team of ten or more salespeople; a company, organization, networking group or association that would enjoy a free workshop?*

Notice the focus is on the client and reinforces that they are happy with you and your product. Secondly, it has begun to set the mindset in their client for the type of referral you are looking for. However, it is a generality on this form. I could be even more specific to insure I will walk away with a name, email, and a cell phone number for a referral that would be interested in my specific product/service.

Who do you know that is a VP of Sales for a large company; someone that hires speakers such as a corporate meeting planner, a trade group, or association that wants to invest in their people and make more money?

Now, I can drill it down even more and add: *Perhaps you know the president or program director of a local or national association like SHRM or a trade group like a chamber or Rotary club. Maybe you know of a corporation that has sales reps that need to polish their phone skills to get more appointments, like a financial firm or a medical supply company. Feel free to contact me with a list of referrals! My job is to make you look good!*

If you aren't sold on the effectiveness of referrals, read what Phil Henderson, President of Henderson Properties, has to say about learning to ask for and use a referral form:

"We hired Tamara as the keynote speaker for our company's annual meeting, and she shared some applicable ways our staff can provide great customer service. She had the team actively engaged in learning, and everyone walked away ready to put what they learned into practice. We also hired Tamara to help us develop some internal documents to improve our overall customer service and sales. These documents included a custom referral form and referral tracking spreadsheet, as we did not already have a referral program in place. We obtained 65 referrals from staff in our first quarter and closed ten of them, resulting in $27,000 of gross revenue. By year end, we obtained 228 referrals, closed 75, and had gross sales of $122,288.89, with another $12,000 about to come in! Each year our revenue has increased! The results would not have been this good without a proactive plan to build our business. Thank you, Tamara!"

> **Since one referral is equivalent to fifteen cold-calls,
> let's start strengthening relationships with
> our existing clients and be smarter in our
> approach to building our business!**

How to Obtain Referral Business

In his book *How to Win Friends and Influence People*, Dale Carnegie wrote, "If you get only one thing out of this book it would be an increased tendency to always see things from the other person's point of view. The only way on earth to influence other people is to talk about what they want and show them how to get it."

> **The key ingredient to getting in the door is
> to appeal to a craving that all human beings
> have, which is a feeling of importance!**

Remember how I asked Mel what she liked about this man she was referring me to and how she went on and on about him? Well, I simply left him a voicemail that said: "Hi Tim, my name is Tamara with Advanced Results, 704-247-8333, 704-247-8333. I got your name and number from Mel Miller and she told me something awesome about you. Call me!"

That was my entire voicemail. Not only did I get a call back, but was invited in for a meeting with his top executives and then was asked to present at their next company event. In the meeting, Tim was shocked that I was even in a meeting with him because he says he rarely calls anyone back and wondered what I did to get in his door? I said I'd not only tell him, but teach his salespeople how to do it when he hired me as his keynote speaker. I got what I asked for!

Once I told Tim about all of the awesome things Mel said about him, Tim called Mel to thank her. Then he thanked her for introducing me to him. The coolest part of all is they blamed all of their happiness on me and I strengthened their relationship with each other.

In the next chapter you will learn what kind of questions I asked Tim to win over the business that the other sales training company thought that they had in the bag.

Remember, the person that can solve the most problems will usually be the winner!

One key ingredient to your success in obtaining the referral business you really want is to position yourself to be "invited in" to a meeting. It is **not** about inviting yourself in to share "what you do." The way to obtain this invitation from a referral is to ask insightful, probing questions that engage your prospect in conversation so that they eventually say "Why don't we meet or why don't you come into the office so we can talk more."

You absolutely do **not** ask for an appointment without having already created value in the eyes of your prospect, which is the mistake so many salespeople often make. You need to learn how to do this by keeping the focus on them, what they want and need and how they will benefit with a relationship with you. You want to position yourself where the prospect asks you what you do **after they are happy** about the nice things you've told them that their friend said about them. It's all about learning and using a smart strategy!

The Referral Script

If you've ever gotten scripts from your company or from a training company and the script was longer than a paragraph, then I can promise you they won't work. In the cold-calling section, I will show you how to write your own scripts. There is nothing wrong with borrowing what you like from someone else, but you have to own it and make it your own. Also, realize it takes one hundred live calls with prospects to determine if a script even works.

The formula for asking for the kind of referrals you really want is:

1. Get your client or center of influence or professional friend feeling happy.
2. Give them a genuine compliment.
3. Ask for the referral and give them a second compliment.
4. Have your "line" memorized and be specific.

"Hi *Tim*, it's Tamara with Advanced Results. What's going great with you today? Your name popped into my head and I wanted you to know that it was so much fun working with you! (Compliment #1). I was wondering who you might know that's super-successful like you (second compliment) that might be open to investing in their sales staff and making even more money as well. Someone like a savvy friend or entrepreneur that owns a business with a team of twenty or more salespeople, a VP of Sales for a large company, (this is your "line" that is personalized for you and the specific referral you are looking for)."

Do not read this as script. Say it conversationally, mentioning their options of the types of people and companies that you want to work with that will jog their memory as to what you do. Remember that your focus is on making them look good before their friends and clients.

Typically, I will get three or four names and their cell phone numbers with this approach. Then I ask "What do you like about them?" I've had a 100 percent call-back rate! We must be smarter in our approach today because people are tired of being sold in a robotic uncaring way.

A generous person will prosper; whoever refreshes others will be refreshed. (Proverbs 11:25)

What **must** you obtain from your client/friend when receiving a referral?

1. The referral's full name
2. Cell phone number
3. What they like most about this person they are referring.

Your sole focus is to make your client look good and be specific about who you want to meet.

Referral Form and Testimonials

By implementing a "standard operating procedure referral form," you can get similar awesome results to what Henderson Properties did and still does. Below is my referral form and what you will notice is that I always ask for a testimonial at the beginning. This is because it gets my clients in a peak state or happy place. You are asking them to think about all the great things that have happened through using your product. If you don't, then you run the risk of getting a downgraded referral and looking like a salesperson. Once they are happy, they are in a better state to think of people that fit your "line" and you will get their referrals.

You have the power to control the emotional state of your clients by learning to ask better questions. If you ask "How are you doing?" nine times out of ten they will go negative. Just shift your question a little to "What's going great for you today? What are you doing with all of that money I made you? What do you love most about your new home?" It changes the entire dynamic of the conversation, and you will be in control.

Remember, you want to be invited to the pool parties, yacht parties, and events where the winners congregate, not the broke networking group meetings. It is the time to step up your game by knowing what you want and who you want to work with so you can be specific when you ask your satisfied clients for referrals.

Testimonials are proof that you are great at what you do. I learned a hard lesson early in my own sales career concerning this important tool. I always thought that people would just give me testimonials because they got such great results. I was wrong. Even though they were satisfied customers, I found you have to actually ask for a testimonial. "Would you please write a testimonial letter based on your awesome results?"

The next step is to follow up a few weeks later to actually get the testimonial from them. Thank them and then simply say "I look forward to our paths crossing again." Then make sure you cross their path again every 3-6 months. Remember, don't love them and leave them. Send out thank you letters for their referrals, and when you get a referral that turns into paid business, send them a $25 Starbucks gift card. Be grateful and show it. Remember, little things mean a lot!

If you want to get vertical referrals, make even more money, and build stronger relationships, simply follow the steps above to appeal to your existing clients' satisfaction and "feelings of importance." If you just apply the simple, effective methods outlined in this chapter, such as obtaining cell phone numbers, getting clear on your target market, conveying compliments, and strengthening relationships, you will be happier and richer.

In the next chapter you will learn how to ask effective questions that establish your value and give you the cutting edge to win over any competition. Change your questions and you will change your life. You must learn how to give people the opportunity to buy versus trying to sell.

tamarabunte

AMERICA'S #1 SALES COACH

What have you learned that you are excited about? Please write a testimonial we can share.

Your Name_____

Company_____

Telephone (cell) _____

Email _____

Who else can we make this happy?

Who do you know that is a friend or entrepreneur that owns a business with a team of 20 or more salespeople, a VP of Sales for a large company, someone that hires speakers such as a corporate meeting planner, a trade group, or association that might be open to investing in their sales team and making even more money? Thank you!

Name_____ Title_____

Company_____

Telephone (cell) _____ Email_____

What do you like most about this person: _____

Name_____ Title_____

Company_____

Telephone (cell) _____ Email_____

What do you like most about this person: _____

Name_____ Title_____

Company_____

Telephone (cell) _____ Email_____

What do you like most about this person: _____

Name_____ Title_____

Company_____

Telephone (cell) _____ Email_____

What do you like most about this person: _____

Wisdom from the Pro-Verbs

▸ In order to procure a referral, you must have built trust with your client through an attitude of service.

▸ Referrals are given because your client trusts you and believes that you will make them look good with their friends and clients.

▸ Since one referral is equivalent to fifteen cold-calls, learn to start strengthening relationships and be smarter in your approach to building your business.

▸ The key ingredient to getting in the door is to appeal to a craving that all human beings have, which is a feeling of importance.

▸ Remember, the person that can solve the most problems will usually be the winner.

▸ Your sole focus is to make your client look good and be specific about who you want to meet.

Ask Yourself...

What kind of referrals am I asking for—traditional or vertical?

Am I about making my clients look good to their friends and clients?

Am I showing how grateful I am for their referrals?

Am I willing to take the time to develop a relationship where my clients trust me enough to give me a referral?

Pro-Verb Action Steps:

Take the referral form given in this chapter and personalize it to fit your business product.

Make a list of all the clients you currently have that love you and your product.

Practice a "script" that will get your client to a happy place using the referral formula.

1. Get your client or center of influence or professional friend feeling happy.
2. Give them a genuine compliment and ask for a testimonial.
3. Ask for the referral and give them a second compliment.
4. Have your "line" memorized and be specific.

Ask for a testimonial and follow up on it.

Make sure you get their name, cell phone number, and find out what they like most about this person they are referring.

Follow up with the referral.

Send a thank you note to each client for their referrals.

Track your results.

Adjust your script as needed.

A generous person will prosper; whoever refreshes others will be refreshed. (Proverbs 11:25)

CHAPTER 7

Establish Value and Earn More Business

*For though the righteous fall seven times, they rise again, but
the wicked stumble when calamity strikes.* (Proverbs 24:16)

Ask Questions that establish your Value

K nowledge is extremely important, but it is only the first step in the
sales process. Just because we understand our own product or service or value it doesn't mean that the prospect does. I can walk into ten
businesses and tell them if they employ and apply three specific techniques
that it will grow their business and make them more money. However,
this does not mean that they will accept, understand, or receive what I'm
actually saying. The only way to have someone understand your value is
to ask them questions.

> ## Effective sales leaders ask many specific questions.

Let's say I'm your boss and I tell you to send a fax, but you don't do
it. Whose fault is it? Mine, because I didn't communicate in a way so that

you truly did receive and understand what I told you to do. That means I have to take responsibility for your lack of knowledge. It is my responsibility to inquire, not the buyer's. You need to control and direct the flow of information to ensure the information was effectively communicated. The only way for me to be sure that you understood the task would be for me to ask you questions.

Just because you have testimonials and lots of information on your product or service **does not** mean that your prospect sees the value. The only way for you to make sure they get it is ask them the right kind of questions. Have you heard the phrase "don't show up and throw up"? It means that if you go on and on about features and benefits you can possibly talk your prospect out of buying and inevitably help your prospect develop new objections.

One of my mentors in business is Duwayne Keller, president of Duwayne E. Keller & Associates, Inc., licensed franchise owner of Dale Carnegie Training in Southwest Florida. He has said over and over, "Don't tell people what you can ask them."

> **You will transform your business by learning how to ask better quality questions instead of just telling people why you are great.**

The questions you ask should establish your value, but if you just tell people your value you risk them not seeing it. For example, when I told my pastor I was angry and I just no longer felt I could trust God, he said, "It's not that you don't trust him, it's that you don't understand him." There's a difference between saying "I don't trust God" and "I don't understand God." So, instead of focusing on "How could God allow this evil thing to happen to me?" I can ask "How will God make me stronger because of this?"

If you get the same objection from multiple people, it's because you haven't learned the lesson yet of how to overcome it. It's about learning the lesson and moving forward. Your questions control your focus, how you think, and how you feel. If you say "Why can't I lose weight?" your mind will answer the question you ask it. You will flood your mind with reasons like it's because of McDonald's and Baskin-Robbins and my mother's cooking. What happens if you asked a better question, like "How can I lose weight and enjoy the process?" Now your mind has to come up with an answer.

If someone says "Cold-calling is hard?" I would respond "Compared to what? Being broke? Which is harder?" This is what we call a state changer. You will make better decisions when you are in a better state of mind, but the only way to get in a better state of mind is to start asking yourself better questions.

I had a one-on-one coaching client that said, "I'm not happy."

I simply replied, "How will you know when you are happy, so I know when we run into happiness in our coaching session?"

She said, "I will be happy when my kids make their beds every morning, when I sell 90 percent of my clients, and when I'm in a loving, committed relationship."

I asked, "Do you know anyone that has all of those three things?"

She answered, "No."

Then I asked, "Why do you want to be unhappy for the rest of your life? Change your rules for what will make you happy. Anytime your happiness relies on someone else's behavior, you will be unhappy most of the time."

This will work with someone who says "I don't have enough money to buy your product/service." Instead of asking "Why not or can I call you back in six months," ask a better question, like "How will you know when you will have enough money?"

That leads us to the next point in making your questions work for you. You need to find out what problems your customer has that they will pay you to solve.

Stump/Hook Questions

In all labor there is profit, but idle chatter leads only to poverty. (Proverbs 14:23)

Some people are needy because they like to talk, but never act. I used to call companies and ask "What are you currently doing for sales training?" This is bad because now they are focusing on who they are using, which isn't me. If I then ask "What made you choose them?" they will answer that question and give me 100,000 reasons **why** they are using their current firm. There will be no way I can win that debate. I learned this the hard way and want you to learn from my mistakes.

You must control the prospect's focus and **never** bring up the competition. Whoever gets the most focus usually wins the debate even if they are not favored. It's all about focus. If I ask you what your toes feel like in your shoes right now, you will probably wiggle your toes because I just directed your focus. Energy flows where your attention goes.

The questions you ask determine what you focus on, and what you focus on controls what you speak. What you speak steers your body to act or to be lazy, and what you act on determines your results.

When someone took advantage of me financially and committed fraud, I felt taken advantage of and mad at God for not protecting me. My mentor said, "Who are you going to be? The angry bitter person or the person that forgives? Will you be what Ferguson, Missouri has become a year after their riots or will you be Charleston, South Carolina after the church shooting where this city forgave?" That question led me to forgiveness, and I was able to move past this paralyzing issue in my life.

I changed my questions, and it
changed my business completely.

Now I can get hired even if a company already hired another sales training company because I know what to ask to establish my value. Here are a few of my "stump/hook" questions:

"If I were to give you a referral and you called my friend three times and they didn't call you back, what do you train your sales staff to say on the fourth voicemail?"

"If we met eight months ago at a networking event, what do you say to me now to get an appointment with me?"

Typically, after you ask two or three "stump" questions, your prospect will invite you in for a meeting. I developed my "stump/hook" questions by asking myself some questions.

*What do **my clients struggle** with eighty percent of the time?*
*What are **their** issues and problems?*

So, in writing your "stump/hook" questions, you must think of what your prospects struggle with and form a question to tap into that pain. You want your prospect to be stumped and have to think about what you are asking them. The question has to establish your value by inferring you have the answer they are looking for. You want your prospect to engage in conversation with you as quickly as possible. Never delay demonstrating value because chances are something more important will come up. They don't yet know why you are important to them. Learn to ask better questions and watch the money flow in.

Questions are the game changer to your sales career.

Every Superhero Has a Villain

> *The wicked is overthrown through his wrongdoing and calamity, but the [consistently] righteous has hope and confidence.* (Proverbs 14:32 AMP)

Batman is one of my favorite superheroes because he's actually human. Every time he goes to save the city or a person from danger, a villain shows up to try and stop him. All of us have a superhero and a villain inside of us. There is a tug of war going on between doing right and doing wrong. It's the seed of greed that can keep us from stepping into greatness. However, what if our intentions are pure and we are working hard, but someone else like a new boss or an old client turns into the Joker and turns against us?

> *Like a muddied fountain and a polluted spring is a righteous man who yields, falls down, and compromises his integrity before the wicked.* (Proverbs 25:26 AMP)

One negative comment from a prospect can cripple our Batman powers and paralyze us. If we can learn how to harness our Batman-like powers, we can defeat every Joker that comes along and not compromise our integrity.

For example, it's natural to fear what we don't understand or feel we are not trained enough. In some cases it's healthy to do so. However, when it comes to sales it's costly to fear cold-calling. It absolutely works. In fact, it's so effective I have built my business on it for the past nine years! Did you know that most businesses fail within the first year? I would argue it could be because they just didn't learn how to pick up the phone, cold-call, and make new friends.

I recently worked with a company where the owner specifically told me they don't cold-call and asked me not to cover "that part" of prospecting with his class participants. First of all, this could have paralyzed my Batman-like powers as it is a vital part of what I teach. However, since I have learned to battle the villain of negativity right up front, I asked him why he would not want to show his team how to build new relationships. It was time for me to dig deeper into this problem if I was going to really bring effective change in his sales department. Carefully read our conversation. So, when I asked about my showing his team how to build new relationships, he answered, "It doesn't work for us and we just focus on referrals."

I then asked him, "Do you have a referral form?"

"No."

I asked, "How many referrals has your team received this past month?"

"I don't know; we don't track that."

"What do you track?" I asked.

"We track appointments."

I then asked, "What's your cancel/no show rate?"

"60 percent."

"How many phone calls do you require your salespeople to make each day?"

He replied, "We don't have a requirement."

"Do you know about how many they make?"

"No."

I then asked, "Do you have a CRM for your company?"

He exclaimed, "Oh yes! We have a custom one!"

"What do you use it for?" I inquired.

"For clients and prospects."

I asked, "What's your follow-up strategy?"

"It's up to the individual salesperson."

"Do you know what that is?"

He again said, "No."

My questions gave me an overview of this company's sales practices and a focus on where some of the problems may be centered. I put together my training program and aimed it at the areas I knew were causing the problems. Fast-forward a few weeks. I'm now in class with seven, 100-percent-commissioned salespeople. I asked them all the same questions that I asked of the company owner. This is where the biggest disconnect exists in many corporations today. As I suspected, the owner didn't have a clue as to what was going on in his own business.

Though the owner didn't think they needed to learn how to make cold-calls, the salespeople begged me to show them how to "cold-call" because they knew it worked but just didn't know how to do it.

I also found out that not one of the seven people used the custom CRM that the company paid for. They used Outlook and a bucket of business cards to follow up with prospects. On top of that, though, the owner said his company was focused on referrals, not one of the seven participants had asked a client for a referral in the last ninety days. They felt they didn't know how and didn't want to come across as sales-y. Nobody tracked their calls, they had zero follow-ups, no strategy, no plan, and blamed their industry for their lack of success.

So, I showed them what to do and then we began a hands-on practical scenario where I could track their activity. Facts are measurable proof, and both they and the business owner needed to know what worked and what did not!

It took them one hour and forty-five minutes to find ten names and numbers of past clients that they could call and ask for a referral. Then it took another hour to write a four-line script of how to ask for a referral that was based on how they could effectively ask for and receive a vertical referral.

Since their current follow-up strategy was to follow up when they remembered, I changed that into a workable system and gave them a specific follow-up structure for each type of call that they made, and showed them how to create a prospecting plan. We created a system rather than the salesperson relying on their **feelings** to dictate their follow-up strategy.

Then they put what they had learned into practice. The results from just the first day of class were phenomenal. Each participant asked and obtained a minimum of five referrals. Three brave souls made ten cold-calls and ended up with a total of nine appointments. Five of those cold-calls resulted in new clients. There was their proof! They couldn't wait for the next day of classes!

You Can't Manage What You Don't Measure

▸ *Would a weight-loss coach track someone's weight by how they feel or by what the scale says?*

▸ *Do you know your numbers?*

▸ *Do you know how many dials it takes to get a live person?*

▸ *How many calls does it take to get an appointment?*

- *How do you bypass the gatekeeper?*
- *Do you know how and when to ask for referrals?*
- *Do you know how often to follow up on a prospect or a past client without stalking them?*

It is utterly impossible to manage a team of salespeople without having any metrics. Time and time again, we have managers leading salespeople out into the sea of possibility and watching them drown. It's sad, but in so many cases the salespeople are the Batman, and the Joker is upper management. It's simply because they do not have the ability or training to see things from the salesperson's perspective. Therefore, they do not have a corporate agenda that includes a smart growth plan.

A true leader of a company or a team doesn't leave luck up to the economy. They make their own luck, they know their odds, and they play the game to win. Many times the leader finds his team just needs fine-tuning. A leader needs to learn how to harness their team's true potential by following a system that has proven results and gets consistent, activity-driven behavior.

If you are the salesperson and really want buy-in and want to grow your sales, ask your VP of sales to make prospecting calls with you for a day to show you how it is done. A true leader goes first!

That being said, I have to add that you need to participate in your own rescue. So many people are waiting for Batman to rescue them from their pain, their financial woes, their company's bad marketing campaign, and from their own inner Joker.

Don't let your current circumstances or other people's beliefs or opinions about you hold you back from what you really want. When you take personal responsibility for the results in your life, you then are in a powerful position to make a new choice to bring about change. When you blame others for why you don't have what you think you should, Rocky Balboa would tell you that is what cowards do and that's not you!

It's not about how many times you fall or how hard you are hit. What matters is how long you stay down.

If you are following the perfect diet plan, but cheat and have a brownie, does that mean the day, the week, and the month are ruined? The loser says, "Oh heck, I just can't lose weight. It's Betty Crocker's fault!" What I want you to do is say, "Okay, I had a brownie, so I will have extra vegetables at dinner." Winners forgive themselves and move on.

> *For a righteous man falls seven times and rises again, but the*
> *wicked are overthrown by calamity.* (Proverbs 24:16 AMP)

Sylvester Stallone is a hero of mine. He sent his manuscript for his *Rocky* movie to over a hundred different companies and was rejected every time. Do you have that kind of tenacity that, if someone says no, you move on to the next person and then the next until you get a yes, or do you falter at the first "No"? Even if you are the victim of someone else's bad choices, own it and move on.

You can lead a horse to water, but you can't make him drink—unless you make him really thirsty!

Someone is always selling someone. The question is, are you being sold on someone's objections or are you convincing them that what you have to offer is better than their excuses? Sell or be sold! You can give a sales presentation and go on and on about how great your product or service is, but that doesn't mean that your prospect is actually going to buy. You have to make your prospect thirsty for what you are selling.

I was at Costco getting all of my usual stuff and they had a demonstration for a blender. Now, I did not want a blender, but I bought it anyway. Not only did I buy it, but I talked several shoppers watching the presentation into buying one as well. What did they do to sell me a blender that I didn't think I wanted? Do you think seeing a presentation of how a blender works made me buy it? Do you think because they went over all of the features and benefits of what that blender has caused me to buy it? No! They asked questions, which created a conviction within me to want to change, and then they convinced me their product was how to bring about that change.

No, I don't have five servings of vegetables per day.

No, I don't have any energy.

Yes, I do drink coffee all day.

I wasn't condemned for eating bad; rather, I was convinced to want to change. They also created pleasure. I saw the end result, which was the fit, happy person eating the fresh fruits and vegetables. I tasted the glorious fruits and vegetables and began to see myself as that fit person.

People buy for two reasons: pain and pleasure. You have to create both for your prospect. In fact, 91 percent of all buying decisions are based on the consequences if they don't buy it. Learning how to ask quality questions will propel your prospects to make the decision to move forward into buying.

The average salesperson will send newsletters, mail brochures, and wait for the marketing department to generate leads. We call this an "Order Taker mentality," meaning they will facilitate a sale that would have occurred anyway. A well-trained professional salesperson will sell someone something that they didn't know they needed or wanted by creating value in something that will solve their problem, and the salesperson will reach out to the prospect and earn the sale.

We must create massive value and solve problems.

I had a friend who needed a financial advisor. She was ready to sign on the line and get her finances in order. She compiled everything she could for the meeting. When she met with the financial advisor, I was present because I was also rating this top salesperson in the office at how well they did with my friend. He made many classic mistakes and did not get the business.

Number one, he didn't ask her any personal questions, so he did not know the real reason she wanted a financial advisor. As a result, he did not take any of her documents. Instead of understanding how serious she was, he wanted to take the perceived classy slow sales approach and said he would take them at their next meeting. I could almost see her excitement dwindle.

Well, there never was a next meeting because his second mistake was he failed to get her cell phone number. He actually called me two months later to get it. If he had taken her financial documents, he would have had all of the information he needed, he would have built trust with her and complimented her on all the work she had done to prepare for their meeting.

My friend was ready to go and prepared to write him a check, but he didn't take it because he was not perceptive enough to see it. I wanted to scream, but it was proof that assumption does not close the deal. Had he asked the right questions and listened to her answers, he could have gotten her to sign on the dotted line while she was right there in front of him and ready to buy. It was like her motivation died at the end of the meeting, and any follow up he did at that point was of no use.

Especially in a case like with my friend, but at almost any sales meeting, if they don't sign up that day, The Law of Diminishing Intent sets in, which means their motivation dies. I recently did a talk for a group of financial folks. The sales manager, while a nice man, just didn't know what he was doing. I'm not sure that the sales team even really knew what they were selling. After my introductory presentation, the team all agreed that they wanted to be professionally trained. The sales manager asked me to share the training options available and then he would decide what they would do for training.

This delay was costly for all involved. The sales manager went out of town before he made the decision. His people are emailing and calling him wondering when training was going to start, but he decided at the last minute they should pay for some of this training. It was a bad sales decision to hit them with a bill two weeks after the fact, so, you guessed it, nobody is getting trained.

Why do I coach only successful people? They are the ones that want to be even better. I tried for years to convert the broke salespeople, wanting to "show them the light" and see that with a little discipline, a little concentrated intentional effort, they can have the BMW, too. Sadly, very few made the conversion. That's why the rich get richer—they want to.

Change Your Questions...Change Your Life

What do your clients really struggle with? What is their pain? You must be the solution to their pain. I was working with a lady in the payroll business. She pretty much had the same pricing as the competition, so she really could only sell customer service. She used to ask:

"What made you decide on your current payroll processor?" Remember, a stump/hook question is created based on what you perceive to be a problem for your customer. So, we worked to find the right stump/hook questions for her.

She discovered that some major issues for Human Resources were checking stubs, not knowing how to use a payroll system to account for an employee's sick and vacation days while being burdened with incoming calls from employees asking how many vacation days they had left for the year. So, now she asks "Do your employees see their vacation and sick accrual balances on their check stubs?" Problem discovered, solved, and the business was hers.

Let's say you're in real estate. So, instead of asking what's important to a client in a house or what they value most, ask them for the three things they "must" have in a home. I was taught that a good attorney will always answer a question with a question. This technique puts it all back on the prospect and now you can qualify if they are really serious. Questions qualify your buyer, not assumptions. Too many salespeople assume the sale without asking any questions, or worse, the buyer is so excited to buy that the salesperson fails to ask questions. Then when the deal falls through they have nothing left to go back to use to sell them because they have no idea what's important to them.

Einstein said, "You can't solve problems by using the same kind of thinking you used when you created them." In the next chapter, we will solve this problem by gaining control of our own lives by gaining control of our thinking.

Wisdom from the Pro-Verbs

- ▸ Questions are the game changer to your sales career.
- ▸ Effective sales leaders ask many specific questions.
- ▸ You will transform your business by learning how to ask better quality questions instead of just telling people why you are great.

▸ I changed my questions and it changed my business completely.

▸ Learn to ask better questions and watch the money flow in.

▸ It's not about how many times you fall or how hard you are hit. What matters is how long you stay down.

▸ You can lead a horse to water, but you can't make him drink— unless you make him really thirsty!

▸ We must create massive value and solve problems.

Ask Yourself...

What is great about this problem versus why do I have this problem?

What has to happen for this problem to be solved?

How will I know when I'm receiving value?

What is the hardest thing I have ever had to overcome?

What pulled me through it?

What did I learn today?

What have I given today?

How can I make God smile even more?

What am I committed to in my life right now?

Pro-Verb Action Steps:

The questions you ask determine what you focus on, and what you focus on controls what you speak. What you speak steers your body to act or to be lazy, and what you act on determines your results. So, practice good sales etiquette.

▸ *Create an emotional bond by asking emotionally based questions.*

▸ *Get people to commit to something before they leave your office.*

▸ *Let them be excited to buy verses you feeling like you are selling them something.*

Have you ever heard a real estate person say "It is my slow season"? That just means they are slow to act in that month because they believe it is slow. Don't buy into that lie. Don't let someone else make your prospect thirsty. You sell them the blender they didn't even know they wanted by pro-actively asking the stump/hook questions!

CHAPTER 8

I'm a Control Freak; Shouldn't I Be Thinner and Richer?

All things are lawful, but not all things are helpful.
All things are lawful, but not all things build up.
(1 Corinthians 10:23)

I remember starting a diet when I was in college, saying "I'm going to plunge into moderation." There is an oxymoron that exists in all of us. It is usually based on the "If / then" lie. If I could just lose fifteen pounds, then I would be happy. If I just make X amount of money, then I will be successful. The problem is anytime we place blame outside of ourselves we lose our power. There is one phrase that outlines the main cause to everyone's problems. It's in the old story we repeat every year, over and over, as to why we don't have what we want.

▸ I'm overweight because everyone in my family is overweight; it's in my genes. *Therefore, I am not responsible.*
▸ I'm not being paid what I'm worth because I didn't go to college, or I did go to college and I'm still not paid what I'm worth. *Therefore, I am not responsible.*

▸ I can't focus on losing weight until after I finish xyz. Therefore, *I am not responsible.*

Many times a "fact" we are basing our rationalization on is really just a belief that we feel so certain about that it takes things out of our control. I had a lady say to me once, "Tamara, it's a fact that I've failed at every diet I've attempted." She has taken on that blame and is now certain that any other diet won't work for her. She sees her attempts as mistakes because she doesn't feel capable of achieving her goal. What's really going on is she is not tapping into her resourcefulness because the story she is telling herself keeps her stuck. She's viewing her attempts as failures, or there is something wrong with her instead of learning a lesson and having a new perspective or thought about what something means.

> *"You must take personal responsibility. You cannot change the circumstances, the seasons, or the wind, but you can change yourself. That is something you have charge of."*
> – Jim Rohn

What you resist facing will persist. In other words, the longer you tell yourself why you can't have something or blame someone else for why you don't have something, the longer you will be faced with the same exact challenges you have been facing. Until you learn a new lesson or change your perspective on your situation, it has control over you. In order to deal with this control issue, we need to get at the root cause.

What if what you want is what's controlling you?

> *"If you don't like something, change it. If you can't change it, change your attitude."* – Maya Angelou

Does that piece of chocolate cake control you? Does that cigarette have power over you? From a biblical perspective, do you have an idol or something that you idolize? Is there anything that you want so badly that you will violate your values to get it?

We consume what we think about. What we think about can consume us if we are not careful.

It never fails that when someone wants coaching to take their career to the next level they also want to lose weight. Even though they are totally different issues, it's the same emotions that are holding them back both professionally and personally. Whether it's Fear of Success or Fear of Failure or any other emotion, once we pinpoint the feeling, we can heal the wound. Too many people try to take emotion out of it and just look at the facts, and that's why they stay stuck. If we want to conquer whatever is holding us back from becoming the best version of ourselves, we must change our mental state.

You can't get where you want to go with the same thinking that got you where you are.

Anthony Robbins says, "If you always do what you have always done, then you will always get what you've always gotten." So, if you want better results, then **you** need to make changes. Lysa Terkeurst wrote a book entitled *Made to Crave – Satisfying Your Deepest Desire with God, Not Food.* Her book was the tipping point for me when I just couldn't seem to overcome the imposing obstacle of losing weight. I've lost the same ten pounds over and over, but the issue really wasn't my weight, it was how food seemed to be controlling me. Anytime we want something more than we want God, it becomes an idol or an obsession. What we need to be obsessing about is God, not food!

What do you wallow in? What abundance do you overindulge in, whether it be the love of money or the love of food? Jesus would say to us, "I want you to give up the one thing you crave more than me and then come, follow me." It brings us back to asking ourselves, "How can I make God smile even more?"

For years I had always wanted to tithe 10 percent to God, but just never seemed to have enough to do it. I always needed (or wanted) the purses, the shoes, the clothes before I wanted to give 10 percent to a church. It's not that I didn't want to give, it's that my priorities were not in alignment. So, when I was in debt over my head, I thought, "Well, it can't get any worse. I might as well start putting God first now because only God can lift me out of this mess." So, I took 10 percent off the gross amount my company brought in and started putting God first.

Our actions speak much louder than our words.

Lysa Terkeurst quoted 1 Corinthians 10:23: "Everything is permissible – but not everything is beneficial." I quote this to myself often as one of my state changers. It helps me focus on the choices that I have rather than the feeling I get that is controlled by the brownie. We all can have power and authority over what might *appear* to be controlling us.

Lysa Terkeurst talks candidly in her book about her thought process and the cycle she'd come to hate and felt powerless to stop. "If I admit my struggle with food to my friends, they might try to hold me accountable the next time we go out. What if I'm not in the mood to be questioned about my nachos *con queso* with extra sour cream? I'll just tell them I'll be starting on Monday, and they'll be fine with it. They don't think I need to make changes. Trouble was, I **did** need to make changes. I knew it. Because this wasn't really about the scale or what clothing size I was; it was about this battle that raged in my heart. I thought about, craved, and arranged my life too much around food. So much so, I knew it was something God was challenging me to surrender to his control."[12]

What I needed to learn was what surrender really looked like. What I discovered is that it's praying every time I found myself craving something other than what is a part of my plan to reach my goal. I had to start doing things God's way.

> *Give ear to my words, O LORD, consider my sighing. Listen to my cry for help, my king and my God, for to you I pray. In the morning, O LORD, you hear my voice; in the morning I lay my request before you and wait in expectation.* (Psalm 5:1-3)

Lysa Terkeurst describes one of her prayers: "God, I want a biscuit this morning. Instead, I'm eating poached eggs. I'm thankful for these eggs, but I'll be honest in saying my cravings for other things are hard to resist. Instead of wallowing in what I can't have, I'm making the choice to celebrate what I can have."

---

[12] Lysa Terkeurst, *Made to Crave – Satisfying Your Deepest Desire with God, Not Food.* Proverbs31.org

Non-negotiable

> *Do not join those who drink too much wine or gorge them-*
> *selves on meat, for drunkards and gluttons become poor, and*
> *drowsiness clothes them in rags.* (Proverbs 23:20-21)

It's funny how when smart people come in for coaching, what they really want is for me to tell them what to do. If someone isn't sure, then I usually point them in the direction to ask someone that has been down the same road that they are on and who has been successful at what they want to achieve.

First things first: who are you spending time with? If all of your friends are overweight and struggling, do you think they will want you to be skinnier than they are? Think about it. Happy people tend to spend time with happy people, and rich people hang out with rich people. It is better to place yourself in an environment that will be the example of what you want to become than to try to change people that are in a similar challenge.

Have you ever been in a relationship where your "friend" really wasn't happy for you if you got a promotion or lost weight or anything that you did to better yourself? I had a friend that was really nice and always helped me out with my baby, but I just felt that there was a competition between us. She didn't make me feel valued because, in the long run, she was actually comparing herself to me and competing with me.

Every time another "friend" got a boyfriend, she would dump me and then when the boyfriend dumped her she would come running back to me. Then, when I got a boyfriend, she dumped me then, too. She was never a true friend because her friendship was based on her rules, which was for her to feel superior to me at all times.

> **A true friend is someone that is there in the good times and the bad, celebrates your wins, and challenges you to become the best version of yourself.**

So, I set a non-negotiable agreement with myself: *"I will only be in a relationship with someone who makes me feel valued."*

Have you ever been lied to by someone? Have you ever put your trust in a person and then they betrayed your trust? Perhaps you need a non-negotiable agreement of "Trust with verification." Maybe it's not a matter of whether you trust someone or not, but that you put enough value on yourself that you don't ever allow someone to break that trust.

Lysa Terkeurst also mentions in her book that for years she identified herself by her circumstances instead of her relationship with God. For years, I defined my identity based on the circumstance rather than on what God thought of me. If a man liked me, then I was likable, and if a man rejected me, then I was not good enough. My circumstances dictated my identity and my worth. I thought if I wasn't "picked" by a man, like a child isn't "picked" to be on the soccer team, that there was something wrong with me.

My non-negotiable agreement with myself had to become: *I was already picked by Jesus, and no man or soccer team captain can take that away from me.*

So, if someone makes you feel less than your true identity, less than what God says about you, why are you spending time with that person?

No weapon that is formed against me shall prosper; and every tongue that shall rise against me in judgment thou shalt condemn. (Isaiah 54:17)

The Power of the Tongue

*Death and life are in the power of the tongue; and they that
love it shall eat the fruit thereof.* (Proverbs 18:21)

This is probably the most powerful of all proverbs because "eat the fruit
of'" is describing that you literally will eat your words. It's like the saying
"you are what you eat." If your words are of lack, loss, or self-loathing, you
will literally become what you speak. The old saying "sticks and stones
may hurt my bones but words will never hurt me" is the biggest lie ever
told! Can you think of a time when someone said something mean to
you? I can. I was called "too tall Tammy" when I was in first grade, and
guess what, I've always had issues with my height. It wasn't until I started
embracing whom God made me and learning to love me that I can now
speak the truth about myself.

We must start speaking life into our future so that we see what God
sees. All we need is in the Bible to begin to speak these words of life to
ourselves. If we are going through a tough time, we aren't to just tell God
how bad it is and wait for him to rescue us. He has already given us peace
and joy and everything else we need to become what he has called us to
be. We need to participate in our own rescue, which means to stop putting
ourselves in situations where we know we will fail. We don't start a diet
then plan on taking our niece and nephew to the local doughnut shop.

*O LORD, you hear my voice; in the morning I lay my
requests before you and wait in expectation.* (Psalm 5: 2-3)

God didn't say, "Tell me all of your problems and then keep complaining." He said, "Lay your requests before me and tell me what you

want, then live in a state of expectation, excitement, and anticipation for the good to come."

Here are truths I tell myself as I live in a state of expectation:

- *I am the righteousness of God in Christ.*
- *God loves me.*
- *I have gifts and talents and abilities.*
- *I am creative.*
- *God is working in this house.*
- *Good things are happening.*
- *I call this a house of peace.*
- *My marriage is solid and strong.*
- *Past, you have no power over me.*
- *I believe my family is healed and whole.*
- *My son is going to grow up and serve God.*
- *All of my children will marry born-again, spirit-filled men/women of God who serve God together and do great things in the earth.*
- *I have favor everywhere that I go.*
- *I have wisdom from God.*
- *God is, I am; therefore, all is well.*
- *All of our needs are met.*
- *We have a surplus of funds.*
- *Every bill is paid early or on time.*
- *I am the victorious child of God.*
- *I am the confident child of God.*
- *I am the loved child of God.*
- *I am the accepted child of God.*

Making a declaration of the truth is speaking the truth based on God's word and leaning on his strength and praying with expectation. You are thanking God and asking for what is promised in his word. The word of God is so powerful that it trumps even those things you have previously considered facts about why you have not achieved your goals. Wouldn't life just be easier to lean on his strength rather than on your own will?

If we rely on just our own strength, that makes God second and we become the rulers of our circumstances. My question to you is, how has that worked out for you so far?

We must be motivated by hope. If we are avoiding something, that is fear. If we are motivated by moving away from something, that is pain. When you stop trying to please people and start trusting that God has your back, you are motivated by hope and are able to move forward and attain your goals. So, what is the formula for this powerful motivation by hope?

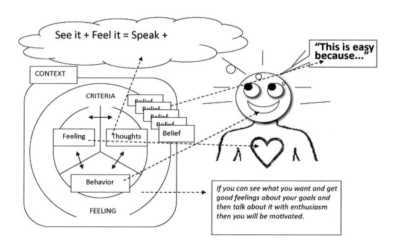

Formula for Motivation[13]

There are two ways people are generally motivated. The "Carrot"—that is, the "thing" out there in the future that you want, like a new car, a dream

---

[13] Michael Bennett created the graphic. He is with Bennett Stellar University.

vacation, or a house. When you create a picture of what you really want and you look or think about that picture of your desire, it gives you good feelings. You tell yourself and others what you want, and you begin to move in the right direction to achieve it.

Motivated people typically focus on the end result. They think about what it is that they want and what it would feel like to have it. They give themselves supporting evidence to enhance and create a stronger belief (reasons) why they can achieve what they want.

The next type of motivation is "the Stick." This means you are motivated "away from" pain rather than motivated "towards" seeking pleasure. For example, let's say you want more money, but find yourself not motivated to go and pick up the phone. That means you might need to focus on what you will miss out on if you don't pick up the phone. You will want to give yourself lots of reasons why not picking up the phone will cause you severe pain.

Typically, when the bank account gets low, you will work hard to get the bank account back to an acceptable level, but then your motivation will wear off again. The solution is to challenge yourself to be more motivated in the area in which you struggle. You want to picture what it would be like to have your goal, thus focusing on the outcome. Some people are more motivated by the carrot and some people are more motivated by the stick.

What you will notice from the diagram is that feelings affect your thoughts and vice versa, and what you think about and feel most of the time shows up in your behaviors. For example, it might be fair to say that if someone does not eat healthy, then they are more likely to feel bad about their eating habits and/or think about how hard it is to eat healthy. They are then in a defeated state. Their behavior is the direct result of their thoughts and feelings.

Strategy for Procrastination[14]

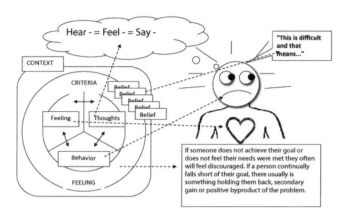

Strategy for.......Procrastination

On the other hand, someone who procrastinates will focus on the steps involved, such as how much time something will take, what it will feel like at the gym to work out, and what other people say about how hard the steps are. The internal and external language is "This is difficult and that means...." They list all the reasons why they shouldn't go to the gym, pick up the phone, or put money in a savings account. Typically, if they procrastinate, they are usually remembering what someone said about a certain situation. That thought makes them feel defeated and then their language supports the negative feelings that they have. We need to learn to focus only on the positive.

The best way to do this and stay motivated is to see your goal (outcome) in front of you. Imagine it in your mind's eye, visualize it, see the colors, smell it, and feel it. Create a vision board to keep your goals in front of you. By making your house a "vision board," you will always be

---

[14] Michael Bennett created the graphic. He is with Bennett Stellar University.

focusing on what you **want** versus what you don't want. See the picture and notice what you look like, what others are saying about you, how you feel, and notice if you can smell or taste anything. Create your destiny by focusing upon your goal and never let go of that picture until you see that goal as a reality. Your imagination will always be stronger than your will.

This can work in the negative as well. For example, food isn't sinful, but if food is what Satan holds up in front of you, he will try to fill your mind with negativity, saying, "You'll never be free from this battle. You will always bounce from feeling deprived when you're dieting to feeling guilty when you're splurging. Victory isn't possible. You aren't capable of self-control with food." At that point, you start to imagine negative things, which, in turn, steer your behaviors.

Apply your heart to discipline and your ears to words of knowledge. (Proverbs 23:12)

It's not about beating ourselves up for not having the discipline to stop eating the chocolate, but the discipline to hear the whisper of the Holy Spirit telling us to walk away. It says in Proverbs that a righteous man falls seven times and rises again, which tells me that when we fall, it's not permanent. We might have a donut, but that doesn't mean the rest of our day is ruined.

When our identity is wrapped up in how we look or how others perceive us, then it's easy to fall and stay down. However, when our identity is not wrapped up in our current circumstances, then we can and will push through. I always tell people that it doesn't matter how many coaches we have because we are all going to get knocked down. That is life. The real question is, *How long will we stay down? 10 minutes? 10 hours? 10 days?*

10 years? If we are cold-calling and someone hangs up on us, how long will it take us to pick up the phone again?

Control the Pictures in Your Head

Emotional fitness is deciding what we want and our feelings will follow. Emotional suicide is letting our feelings dictate our choices. It is vital that we do **not** define ourselves by the numbers on the scale or whether someone likes us or not. What defines us is our obedience to God's word. Let's find our joy and happiness in God. Too many people fall prey to the illusion of "If/then" disease. We must first feel successful, joyful, and happy **before** we get the tangible result because our weight and our bank account do not determine our happiness. If we falsely correlate the two, then we will be disappointed.

We must be able to control our mindset. We will crave what we focus on. Our imagination is stronger than our will. That means that if we imagine having a piece of cake and we keep thinking about how much we want it, our imagination of that piece of cake will override our will not to eat it. This is the place where so many people fall off the wagon and delve into the guilty pleasure of what they say they don't want to control them any longer.

We must learn to control our imagination and picture what we want rather than think about what we don't want and "shouldn't" be having. If we make our goals a must by **making a real decision as to what we want** rather than stating a preference or a wish, then we control the pictures in our head. At that point, we will we start to make real progress.

I know that the only one responsible for me is me. God is on my side to help me, but only if I allow God to help and begin to follow the wisdom of his word to make my choices. What will you choose today?

A wise man is strong, and a man of knowledge increases power. For by wise guidance you will wage war, and in abundance of counselors there is victory. (Proverbs 24:5-6)

Wisdom from the Pro-Verbs

▶ We consume what we think about. What we think about can consume us if we are not careful.

▶ You can't get where you want to go with the same thinking that got you where you are.

▶ Our actions speak much louder than our words.

▶ A true friend is someone that is there in the good times and the bad, celebrates your wins, and challenges you to become the best version of yourself.

▶ True faith is waiting in expectation! – *Tamara Bunte*

▶ I know that the only one responsible for me is me.

Ask Yourself...

Is there anything I want so bad that I will violate my values to get it?

Is there anything I want more than God in my life?

What am I attempting to do in my own power but failing at?

Who is controlling my identity?

Which motivation works best for me, the carrot or the stick?

Wouldn't my life be easier if I just learn to lean on God's strength rather than on my own will and power?

Pro-Verb Action Steps:

True faith is waiting in expectation! Explain the difference between hoping and expecting:

Hoping is _____

Expecting is _____

Are you hoping or expecting? _____

God is on my side to help me, but only if I allow God to help. It is my choice.

What will you choose today? _____

One of the ways I can help rescue myself is to work on the way I talk about myself to myself.

If you are always late, start saying, "I am awesomely punctual."

If you don't have the resources you need, then start saying, "I am resourceful."

If you feel weak, then start saying, "I move forward with the strengths I have."

If your feelings get in your way, then say, "I walk by faith."

What other rephrasing do I need to start doing? _____

One of the best ways to gain control of my thinking and stay motivated is to see the outcome of reaching my goal in front of me. Describe your goal: _____

Imagine it in your mind's eye, visualize it, see the colors, smell it, and feel it.

Now create a vision board to keep your goals in front of you.

*Make your house a "vision board" so you will always be focusing on what you **want** versus what you don't want.*

Create your destiny by focusing upon your goal and never let go of that picture until you see that goal as a reality.

CHAPTER 9

Cold-Calling Made Simple

Trust in the LORD with all your heart and lean not on your own understanding; in all your ways acknowledge him, and he will make your paths straight. (Proverbs 3:5-6)

Why It Works and How to Do It

The soul of the sluggard craves and gets nothing, but the soul of the diligent is made fat. (Proverbs 13:4)

If anyone tells you that cold-calling doesn't work, it just means they have a bad attitude about it. A bad attitude always foreshadows poor results. Cold-calling is extremely effective if you are good at it. If you don't know how to do it, then you will develop a bad attitude about it because your potential customers will hang up on you. If you get hung up on, that means you were not good at articulating your value over the phone and your potential customer just sold you on why they won't do business with you.

If you are going to be great in sales, then you must be great at **all** areas of sales. If anyone tells me that "They won't cold-call," that tells me they are unwilling to make new friends.

If you are in sales, you are
"a professional friend finder."

If you "don't believe in cold-calling," you might be losing out on a lot of sales, money, and new friends. Too many sales gurus say that cold-calling is dead. The truth is, they just don't want to do it.

How do you help a salesperson who is striving for $100,000 a year but doesn't get leads from his company? What does he do all day? He begins by calling on past and current clients and asking for referrals. What should he do after he has called all of his existing clients? Networking and follow-up with whomever he has met. Then he **must** move to cold-calls and make new friends.

Wealth from get-rich-quick schemes quickly disappears;
wealth from hard work grows over time. (Proverbs 13:11)

Let me be blunt: cold-calling is hard work. You will have moments of doubt. Some people will not be nice. However, I have learned how to do cold-calling successfully and will teach you how you can as well. I built my business on cold-calling, and it totally works! Your input determines your output. If you aren't making cold-calls, you are missing out on a lot of potential sales and income.

However, you have to start out with the mindset; it is not about you and how much money you can make.

> **You have to realize that calling is not about you;**
> **it's about solving a problem for the person**
> **on the other end of the phone.**

Let's say you are in financial services. The problem is that most financial advisors have not been taught how to effectively make cold-calls. They simply don't know what questions to ask to spark intrigue. If they say to the prospect, "The reason for my call is to meet with you so I can re-evaluate your financial plan," the prospect will most likely say, "I'm all set." Asking a better question might help that financial advisor engage in conversation and actually get an appointment.

No matter what it is you are selling, the secret to success is to ask questions that will help you discover and then solve your client's problems. This means you need to do your homework before you make the call. In the case of the financial advisor, I have confirmed with a multitude of financial advisors that rarely do homeowners ever put down a few hundred dollars more towards the principal on their mortgage payment.

So, what if an advisor asked, "Have you ever considered paying a few hundred dollars more a month to pay off your mortgage in half the time? Has anyone ever told you that would massively lower the amount of interest paid on your home if you do that? Have you ever looked at how much you pay each month towards your principal versus towards your interest?"

This question will "stump" this prospect 80 percent of the time and hook them into considering such a great idea. Once you have piqued their interest with a great stump/hook question or two, you can engage them in a conversation to begin to discover how you can help them solve their financial problems. If you can't engage them in a meaningful conversation and establish your value, quite frankly, you don't deserve their business.

Sales Prospecting and Cold-Calling

Webster's dictionary **definition** of **sales prospecting** is the process of reaching out to potential customers in hopes of finding new business. **Prospecting** is often the first part of the **sales** process that comes before follow-up communication, lead qualification, and **sales** activity.

A **Cold-Call**, which is a verb, insinuates the action is to make an unsolicited call on someone by telephone or in person in an attempt to sell goods or services. It is the solicitation of potential customers who were not anticipating such an interaction. Cold-calling is a technique whereby a salesperson contacts individuals who have not previously expressed an interest in the products or services that are being offered, as opposed to warm-calling received through a lead or a referral. Cold-calling typically refers to phone calls, but can also entail drop-in visits such as with door-to-door salespeople. In finance, cold-calling can refer to a method through which brokers obtain new business by making unsolicited calls to potential clients.

Prospecting 101

> *"Prospecting is to sales what seeds are to a garden. If we don't plant seeds, we won't get flowers. The more seeds we plant, the more flowers we get."* –Dale Carnegie

You have to identify the different types of people in your database. You typically have two major categories, clients and leads. You can organize your clients based on what they buy and your leads based on how you can obtain business.

These five categories about how I make my money are:

Client-Product: People that have bought my book and CD products.

Client-Corporate: People that hire me for customized in-house sales training.

Client-Coaching: People that hire me for one-on-one coaching.

Client-Classes: People that register for a public class like Prospecting Mastery.

Client-Keynotes: People that hire me for a paid speaking engagement.

Break your clients into categories based on how you make money and then set a goal per category group. Maybe I want to sell 200,000 books and do 100 Keynote presentations, and maybe I only want to take on 10 one-on-one coaching clients. This way I can set goals based on the income I want to achieve and diversify what I sell for cross-sell opportunities.

The next group is *leads*:

Lead-Product: People that potentially want to buy my products.

Lead-Corporate: People that potentially want to hire me for customized training.

Lead-Coaching: People that are potentials for one-on-one coaching.

Lead-Classes: People that potentially want to take my classes.

Lead-Keynotes: Companies that want to potentially hire me to speak.

Lead-Referrals: Referrals obtained.

Lead-Internet/Ad: Leads that came through online.

Lead-Attendees: People that were in the audience from a speaking engagement.

Lead-Cold-Call: A list that we bought (Target Market).

So, where do you start? First, call your current clients and ask them what they like about you! This is great to do when you start your day and will put you in a peak state. Then simply ask them for a referral. No sense in making cold-calls if you haven't talked to people that already love you.

Next, call past clients to renew your connection or place a re-order or cross-sell/upsell and to ask for referrals.

If you get an internet lead, call them as soon as possible. They are hot and usually ready to buy.

The next group would be people that said "No" in the past. Maybe they changed their mind, maybe their old boss with a bad attitude has retired. Plus, you always want to start with people that you've called a few times but who haven't called you back yet.

Remember, you have to call people five to twelve times to have an 80 percent conversion rate. If you've pitched people and they haven't called you back, it's time to practice better sales etiquette. Refer to previous chapters for effective voicemail techniques.

Always leave a voicemail. Calling and not leaving a message is stalking. You can now mix up your calls between "warm" calls in the other categories based on how you make money. I will typically call referrals on Tuesday afternoons so that I have structure to my month. This includes calling to ask for referrals and calling to actually obtain referral business.

Now you want to add in cold-calling. However, don't just call anybody. Figure out your target market. Remember, you don't want to be seen as a commodity; you want to present yourself as the best and the only real option.

How to Get Referrals from a Cold-Call

Rule #1: Never ever call a company and ask who the manager is and then ask to be transferred. You will be red flagged, and I promise you it will go right to voicemail because that tactic has been attempted by three other salespeople every day for the past decade. To get in, you need to do something different. First, call them and say you are updating your records and simply ask, "Who is the VP of Sales or the owner or whomever is the person that is the decision maker?" Here is a trick: when the gatekeeper tells you this, ask him/her what do you like about the VP of sales. For example, "Is she/he a cool person?" Ask some more questions about the VP because you are collecting valuable information.

A few hours later or a day later, call the VP and leave the referral voicemail (discussed previously), and it becomes like a referral call, much warmer than pitching your product on voicemail. Plus, you are building a relationship. Have you ever heard someone say "I got too many compliments today"? Remember, we have to be classy, smart, and skilled to earn the business. People are too jaded today to just hear a pitch like "Let's meet and shake hands, so I can tell you what I do." It just doesn't work. We have to get decision makers to call us back so that we can establish value.

Important to note that our potential clients are everywhere. Let me tell you how I met Bill Gallagher with The Superior School of Real Estate in Charlotte, NC. I was on a date and we were having lunch right next to the Superior School of Real Estate. He suggested I call Bill, so I did. I've been working with them for eight years. I also got a lead into the United States Army from being on The Superior School's website—good just keeps flowing.

> **Never assume that the person in front of
> you can't refer you to your best clients.**

Rule #2: Do not pitch your product or service to the gatekeeper. They are not on your team, and they are terrible at pitching your product/service to the true decision maker.

The gatekeeper is not your friend.

The gatekeeper wants to know your name, company, and sometimes what the call is in reference to. It's none of their business and under no circumstances should you give them any information other than your name and company name.

You have two reasons that you are calling and **only** two reasons:
1. The gatekeeper will ask, "What's this in reference to?"
   You respond, "Oh, the XYZ Company."
   They will say, "Okay, hold please."
   Not once in ten years has a gatekeeper asked me about the XYZ Company.
2. The second question the gatekeeper will ask is the reason you are calling.
   You respond, "It's personal."
   That's it. That's all you say.

Another tactic is to give them this information up front with a very high sense of urgency and say, "Hi ____ it's Tamara with Tamara Bunte, Inc.. Will you let John know I'm on the line? I'll hold. Thank you."

One of my favorite ways is, "Hi ____, is John in, by chance?"

The key is "by chance" because it presupposes that you've already talked to John. If you use the word "available" you are average and untrained as a professional salesperson. If you say "available," the gatekeeper will automatically reply, "What's this in regards to?"

If you are really good, you will obtain the decision maker's cell phone number from the gatekeeper. It doesn't always happen, but it happens more often than not.

You sound like you are John's friend and say, "Is John in, by chance?"
Gatekeeper says, "No."

Your response is, "Oh, how did I miss him? You know what, I'll just send him a quick text. What's his cell again?"

The heart of the wise instructs his mouth and adds persuasiveness to his lips. (Proverbs 16:23)

The gatekeeper is friends with your prospect, and if they are a loyal friend they will do what's in their boss's best interest, not yours. Once the decision maker actually buys from you and becomes a client, you become friends with the gatekeeper. You are to treat the gatekeeper as a top-notch client once they become one. Until that time, learn to play your cards right.

Cold-Call Scripts – Become a Professional Friend Finder

"An ounce of action is worth a ton of theory."
– Ralph Waldo Emerson

You have twenty seconds to sell yourself in a cold-call. If you can't articulate your value and what you offer and why they should buy in twenty seconds, they will hang up, guaranteed. What do we say in those precious twenty seconds?

The purpose of a cold-call is to generate interest, and if you are really good, you will get invited in for an appointment. The purpose of a cold-call is not to close a sale. The goal is to qualify, get information, and schedule an appointment.

The biggest mistake most salespeople make is going right for the appointment and providing no value. They want to get the appointment so bad that they end up shooting themselves in the foot. You want people to buy when they are hungry, but on a cold-call they don't even know that they are hungry. So you have to entice them with the appetizer, then the meat, and top it off with dessert. Everyone knows that a good server always starts with the dessert order. Why ask them what they want for dessert when they are already full? When they buy one thing, they will buy everything – sell everything or live paycheck to paycheck.

One of the reasons I was successful when I worked for Tony Robbins was I knew that when they buy one thing, they will buy the package. I'd get the order when they were hungry, not two weeks later after they had eaten.

**Sales is all about control. If you lose
control, you lose the prospect.**

Here are some sample scripts that have worked for me over the years. Feel free to modify these if you wish, but start with these because they are proven to work.

1. *Hi, John, it's Tamara with Tamara Bunte, Inc. The purpose of my call is to see if you are open to inviting a guest speaker into your next sales meeting? Are you a member of the _____ Chamber? We just coached their sales staff to increasing their prospecting skills, and since we trained their sales staff, they've seen on average a 50 percent increase in their production goals year over year. Maggie is the sales director over there. She's awesome! Do you know her?*
   If we could do just half of that for your sales team, would you be willing to host a guest speaker at your next sales meeting?

2. *Hi, John, it's Tamara with Tamara Bunte, Inc. We are offering complementary one-hour sales training workshops to increase your team's performance. Perhaps you would like to have your team evaluated*

on their effectiveness in the top ten skills based on top income earners. How many people do you have on your sales team?

To be sure I'm not wasting your time, tell me, do you have a standard for how many dials per day your sales team makes? (Stump question) John's Response: Um um um.

If I could make your life easier, what are the top two things you would want to enhance with your sales team?

Response: Tamara, why don't you come in so we can talk?

Set the appointment and make sure to **get their cell phone number!**

3. *Objection: "Oh, we are all set."*

   "I can appreciate that, but would your sales guys tell you that they are satisfied with their current income? Why don't you buy them lunch, and I'll come in and test their abilities, fine-tune their skills, and give them some motivation?"

4. *Objection: "We have in-house trainers."*

   "I hear what you are saying, but do you know how many advisors the president has?

   "No."

   "Clearly not enough, right?"

   "Hahaha."

   "But seriously, (insert stump questions)."

5. *Objection: "We're satisfied."*

   "Do you and your sales staff deserve more?"

   "We are here in _____ and are servicing our community business owners by helping them to increase their sales staff performance to make even more money. We typically will come back every six months to a year for further professional development. Would you be open to attending one of these sessions?" (You are building a relationship because everyone buys eventually.)

The process:

- ▸ Identify yourself (first name only) and the purpose of your call.
- ▸ Make a pitch with a real testimonial or just state why you are calling.
- ▸ Ask your first "Stump/hook" question as soon as possible.
- ▸ Ask the next two "Stump/hook" questions.
- ▸ Wait for them to invite you in for an appointment or lead with an assuming the sale question like, "When are you in the office or when does your sales team meet?"
- ▸ Handle objections, if they even come up.
- ▸ Get a day/time on the calendar and send a calendar invite!
- ▸ Get the **cell** phone number from the Decision Maker and text them the day before the meeting and ask how they would like their coffee.

With the fruit of a man's mouth his stomach will be satisfied; He will be satisfied with the product of his lips. (Proverbs 18:20)

Why People Don't Call You Back

Prospects and clients don't call you back because they can't find your phone number. Yes, even if you cold-call them nine times and then you reach them on the tenth call, they will say, "Oh, I was meaning to call you. I couldn't find your number."

You must learn to follow the system of sales, which means that if people don't call you back because they are busy, you must call them. Eighty percent of business will come after the seventh voicemail.

Think of yourself as the head of customer service. Would you call someone for the fourth time and say "I haven't heard from you, so I'm assuming you're not interested; you can call us if we can help you"? If you did, you would be fired from your position.

Never ever make it their responsibility to call you to tell you if they are interested. You must keep calling them and act like it's the first time you have called them. Always be nice, pleasant, and positive. Always start from the beginning, assume everyone is cold even if they are warm.

The last and ultimate reason they haven't called you back is because at this time they do not see enough perceived value to return your call. So, that means you have to get better at your pitch. You have to figure out better stump/hook questions. You have to give them better reasons why they should buy from you right now!

The power lies within you! Be the best!

This is the kind of testimonial you want:

Hi Tamara,

I wanted to share the GOOD NEWS with you about our success with cold-calling.

Before we met you, our team was not cold-calling on a consistent basis. We were also not hitting our monthly production sales goal consistently. Since your class, we've seen on average a 50% increase in our production goals year over year.

Brenda, who has always been a strong team member since she joined us, has not only consistently hit her goal each month, she has seen a 15% increase in her sales over last year. She is already at 97% of her annual goal, and we have 4th quarter to go!

Lee, who joined our team in January, is KILLING his production goals! Lee is at 95% of his year-to-date production goal. He has practically doubled his monthly production goal four out of the last eight months.

Both Brenda and Lee have met and exceeded their monthly and quarterly goals, and it's paid off BIG for them.

Our two newest team members, Matt and Lauren, have quickly filled their pipeline due to cold-calling and are hitting their production goals on schedule. Matt was at 141% of his goal last month, and Lauren is actually at 195% of her goal this month!

We are meeting and exceeding our production goals. COLD-CALLING WORKS!

Thank you for your support and encouragement!

~ Maggie[15]

I have seen a 50% increase in my income over the last two years since taking Tamara's Prospecting Mastery Class. I'm not necessarily working harder, just smarter. Roughly 80-90 percent of my income comes from that 8th to 11th phone conversation with someone looking for the services I provide. – John Thompson

Wisdom from the Pro-Verbs

▸ If anyone tells you that cold-calling doesn't work, it just means they have a bad attitude about it.

▸ If you are in sales, you are "a professional friend finder."

▸ You have to realize that calling is not about you, it's about solving a problem for the person on the other end of the phone.

▸ Never assume that the person in front of you can't refer you to your best clients.

▸ The gatekeeper is not your friend.

▸ Sales is all about control. If you lose control, you lose the prospect.

[15] Thanks to the Charlotte Chamber for investing in their team. If you are in Charlotte, I encourage you to join at: www.charlottechamber.com

Ask Yourself...

What has been my attitude about cold-calls?

How has it changed since I read this chapter?

Am I ready to become a professional friend finder?

Do I present myself as the best and the only real option to my prospects?

Can I convey my value in twenty seconds?

Pro-Verb Action Steps:

Prospecting 101: You have to identify the different types of people in your database. You typically have two major categories, clients and leads. You can organize your clients based on what they buy and your leads based on how you can obtain business.

1. Call your current clients and ask them what they like about you.
2. Call past clients to renew your connection, place a re-order, cross-sell/upsell, and ask for referrals.
3. If you get an internet lead, call them as soon as possible.
4. Call the people that said "No" in the past.
5. Do your cold-calling after you figure out your target market.

Cold-Calls 101:

- ▲ Remember, you never pitch to a gatekeeper.
- ▲ Make sure you know who you are calling. You must have a name to run the script.
- ▲ Know who your decision makers are.
- ▲ Never pitch anything on voicemail.
- ▲ Okay, time to write your own script. Take the parts of the samples I have given you and design your own based on an upcoming cold-call you are going to make.

▲ Include answers to possible objections you have experienced in the past.

▲ Make sure you have at least three stump/hook questions specific to the product or service you are selling.

▲ Make sure you have done your research on this contact and the company he or she works for.

▲ Make sure you give your cell phone number and try to get theirs if you do not connect directly to the decision maker on your first call.

CHAPTER 10

Emotional Fitness – Mindset Makeover

A joyful heart makes a cheerful face, but when the heart is sad, the spirit is broken. The mind of the intelligent seeks knowledge. (Proverbs 15:13-14)

How do you pick up the 5000-pound phone? You first must want to learn how to be good at it. If you don't want to do it, chances are you will make excuse after excuse not to. "Willing" yourself to do it isn't the best strategy either because your imagination will trump your will every time. If the picture in your head is of someone yelling at you and hanging up on you, you will find a way to opt out of making the calls. It is a self-fulfilling prophecy.

When I coach people, I take them back in time in their mind to a bad cold-calling experience and help them change their perception of that past experience. There is usually a lesson that needs to be learned in order for the person to move past the actual event and move forward. There is no sense in speaking an affirmation to themselves while they still internally don't believe it. All that will do is make the pain of a past experience even greater.

The key in real behavior change is to fill yourself up with what you would rather have so you will want to execute the task at hand. It's impossible to make a successful cold-call if you are feeling like you're a failure at sales. Imagine watching yourself play out your last cold-call, but this time take on the beliefs, behaviors, and energy of someone that likes and is good at cold-calling and prospecting and model them. There is no sense in reinventing the wheel.

The key is to have the right resources and emotions to fill yourself up with. If you are shy, then you want to be able to get resourceful and be confident. The easiest way to do this is to think of a time when you were confident, then another time, and then another, and you will notice that you feel totally confident. Change your mind, which changes your focus, which will change the outcome. There are no unresourceful people, only unresourceful states of mind.

**Success is not always about knowing more,
it's about being in a resourceful state of mind.**

Everything is energy. If you want to experience a new reality, find a person that has what you want and model their energy.

"Match the frequency of the reality you want and you cannot help but get that reality. It can be no other way. This is not philosophy. This is physics." – Albert Einstein

What most people just don't get is that you must first assume the feeling of the desire you want. Fake it until you make it. I had a friend that said to me, "I just don't feel good in my own skin. I don't think I can feel pretty until I lose twenty pounds." What she must do is shift her energy to feeling thin now. If she doesn't, even when she does get the weight off she will still feel fat. What will guide her to actually getting the weight off faster would be to feel thin and act thin and then she will be thin.

It's the same thing with salespeople who say "Once I have x amount of dollars then I will feel successful." That does not work. You must feel successful first, then you will attract success. You have to control your mindset and focus it on what you want to manifest. You cannot focus on lack and expect abundance.

You attract what your belief system supports.

Counteracting Disempowering Beliefs

In order to change a belief, you need to have new references and reasons to support it. Once you start to change your thinking, you might find that your mind gets flooded with old disempowering beliefs. That's natural. It's like a test asking you if you really want to change. To counteract these disempowering beliefs, you need to move them out of your active files and replace them with empowering beliefs.

I did this by imagining a folder on my desktop computer. That folder is on the left side of my "mind" screen and is called "Things I no longer believe." I place a mental picture that represents something I no longer believe in, like Santa Claus, on my folder. Anytime an old belief comes up that I no longer choose to believe, I picture myself typing it up and dragging it into that folder.

Now, on the right side of my mind screen, I create a new folder that says "Things I know to be true." I think of my dog Scoobie. I know that she loves me and nothing will take that away, so my new folder has a picture of Scoobie on it. Every time I have a new empowering belief come up, I type it up and drag it into that folder.

I teach salespeople to take this a step further and imagine someone they view as successful in the area in which they are trying to build new beliefs. Then imagine stepping into that person and borrowing from them their beliefs and modeling their energy.

> *Better is a dish of vegetables where love is than a fattened ox served with hatred.* (Proverbs 15:17)

Overcoming Opposition

If you feel like you just can't get above a problem or can't seem to accomplish that goal you've set year after year, or there is that one person that haunts you with negative things that they've said in your past, then it's time to be set free! You can escape the limitations these thoughts have put on you. You must begin by accepting the truth that no weapon formed against you will prosper because God has given you what you need to combat these negative thought patterns and mindsets.

> *We are destroying speculations and every lofty thing raised up against the knowledge of God, and we are taking every thought captive to the obedience of Christ.* (2 Corinthians 10:5)

Don't worry about the haters. They are just angry because the truth you speak contradicts the lie they live.

Is there anything worse than seeing a guilty person get away with murder? This can definitely incite feelings of anger. The angrier someone becomes, the deeper the hurt that person has. We all know that getting angry at a guilty person doesn't change the situation. However, what if you are dealing with a situation that is so difficult that you wish God would anoint you with the privilege of seeking justice? How do you deal with the anger and the injustice you feel? I believe the deeper the valley, the higher the peak.

A fool always losses his temper, but a wise man holds it back.
(Proverbs 29:11)

Revenge is another story. Revenge is when you want the other person to suffer your pain. In this case, you must pray that God will soften your heart and ask him to help you see the other person as he sees them or why they did what they did to you.

Now, the wrong is still there, but here is a suggestion a nun gave me that really works. She said, "I want you to pick out two scarfs and imagine all of the names of the people that have hurt you are written on one scarf. Put it on. How does it feel?" In my case, it felt hard and heavy. Then she said, "Put God's goodness and grace on the other scarf and put that on. How does that scarf feel?" Each day, you and I have a choice as to which scarf we will put on. The choice we make may affect how the day progresses.

Let God take on the hurts and injustices and realize every setback is a set up for something better.

The Scorpion and The Frog

There once was a frog and scorpion. The scorpion asked the frog for a ride on his back to cross the river because scorpions cannot swim. The frog said, "I will not let you ride on my back. You will sting me because you are a scorpion. If you sting me, I will die." The scorpion said, "I just need a ride.

I won't hurt you. You will be helping me get across the river." So the frog agreed, but when they were half way across the pond, the scorpion stung the frog! The frog said, "Why did you do that? Now we will both die!" The scorpion said, "That's what I do. It's just who I am." The scorpion just didn't have the character to do the right thing.

Do you ever find yourself expecting people to do the right thing, but continually find yourself let down? We assume that if someone holds a high position they will automatically do the right thing. Sadly, true moral character is eroding around us today. It's not just about choosing God's way, it's also about discerning the people that might be pretending to be our friends. We have the ability within us to rise above the moral decay and conduct our life and our business in an ethical and honest manner. It is our choice.

> *For His divine power has bestowed on us **[absolutely]** **everything necessary for [a dynamic spiritual] life and godliness**, through true and personal knowledge of Him who called us by His own glory and excellence. For by these He has bestowed on us His precious and magnificent promises [of inexpressible value], so that by them **you may escape from the immoral freedom** that is in the world because of disreputable desire, and become sharers of the divine nature.*
> (2 Peter 1:3-4 AMP emphasis added)

The Bible tells us that the rain falls on the just and the unjust, which means bad stuff is going to happen. The difference is we have more resources with God on our side to handle life's curveballs. We just need to remember that and act accordingly.

*Thou I walk through the valley of death I will fear no evil;
for thou art with me; thy rod and thy staff they comfort me.*
(Psalm 23:4 KJV)

Emotional Intelligence

Emotional Intelligence (EQ) is one's ability to identify, evaluate, control, and express emotions. When someone has a high EQ it means they have the ability to understand, empathize, and connect with people around them. It is, however, totally different from Intellectual Intelligence (IQ), which is used to determine academic abilities. One's EQ will trump one's IQ when it comes to dealing with life's curveballs.

Emotional fitness is defined as someone that lets their choices dictate their emotions. Emotional suicide is letting your emotions dictate your decisions. Someone with a high EQ will face a problem and see it as an opportunity to grow. They will use the negatives as a teacher to learn from. Someone with a low EQ will tend to channel their energy on the conditions of their life and blame people, places, and things for their circumstances rather than taking personal responsibility for their results.

It is only when someone participates in their own rescue that they start to see a change in their life conditions. The way to do this is to become more emotionally fit. The Emotional Quotient Assessment breaks down your emotional intelligence into four categories.

The first three are about intrapersonal emotional intelligence, which is the ability to understand yourself and how you interact with yourself.

Self-Awareness is the ability to recognize and understand your moods, emotions, and drives as well as their effect on others.

Self-Regulation is your ability to control or redirect disruptive impulses and moods and the propensity to suspend judgment to thinking before acting.

Motivation is a passion to work for reasons that go beyond money or status and a propensity to pursue goals with energy and persistence.

These all build on each other as it becomes difficult to self-regulate emotions you are not aware of. The last two are interpersonal emotional intelligence, which is about what goes on between you and others.

Empathy is your ability to understand the emotional makeup of other people.

Social Skill is a proficiency in managing relationships and building networks.

Once you take the assessment, you can then pick where you scored lowest on your scale and pick two or three of the suggestions to start to raise your emotional intelligence.

I had a client that took the assessment and scored almost a ten on all levels except self-regulation. She said she had been aware of how she was feeling, but had a tendency to blame people for her erratic moods. She realized that she needed to work on her ability to control or redirect disruptive impulses and moods, and to suspend judgment before acting. She also noticed that following a diet plan was difficult because, when she would get frustrated or angry, she just gave into whatever food was in front of her. She became aware that she really needed to work on how she responded to stressful situations, be more disciplined and unwavering in her decisions, and not to let her emotions control or dictate what she acted on.

If your **self-awareness** is low, you might not be aware of what you are feeling and why you are feeling a certain way.

If your **motivation** is low, you are motivated by compliance rather than an intrinsic motivation to go above and beyond the status quo.

If your **empathy** and **social skills** are low, you will experience a great deal of trouble connecting with your prospects.

People buy emotionally and then back it up logically. If you sell based on facts, you will find that you run into the dreaded "price" objection. Seeing things from the customer's point of view is what will build your ability to empathize even more. **Empathy** is the ability to experience the feelings of another person and being able to put yourself in their shoes, so to speak. It is different from sympathy, which is caring and understanding for the suffering of others and acknowledging another person's hardships.

Empathy is when you are truly seeing things from another person's perspective, which makes you connect with people on a deeper level. What can hold us back from being more empathetic is having too much to deal with in our own lives and not having much more to give.

> **It's true that people don't care how much you know until they know how much you care.**

What tends to bring a low score in **social skills** is when we focus on our agenda above our client's agenda, focusing on a transactional sale verses a relationship sale (long term relationship), and being persuasive in conversation. If you wish to take the Emotional Intelligence Assessment, contact me at www.TamaraBunte.com.

Minimalism –The Enemy of Excellence

Minimalism is an infectious disease that is scripted as a mentality of "What's the least I can do and still get by?" It is a disease of the mind with a mentality of "have to" versus "get to." It is the reason depression is on the rise and suicide is so prominent. People that might be on the verge of it are working, but are distracted by life's "to do's," so they are not maxing out at their potential.

The question becomes, "Have you trained your brain to become the best version of yourself, or are old beliefs (things people said or did that held you back in the past) still controlling the voice inside your head today?"

A worker's appetite works for him, for his hunger urges him on. A worthless man digs up evil. (Proverbs 16:26-27)

Do you dig up memories of people from your past that hurt you and relive those experiences? Do you replay old hurts over and over again? Worse yet, do you continue to attract the same types of people into your life that don't celebrate who you really are? If you don't change your perspective on past events and see a new hope for the future, you may repeat the same story over and over. That story is usually what holds people back. "Moving forward" is reminding yourself that every day is a new day with new opportunities and new possibilities. Isn't it time to write a new story with a positive and productive ending?

I used to despise prospecting, but I turned my misery into my mission to help others to see the light. I did it through changing my perspective and learning new ways to approach it from people that were good at it and enjoyed it. I modeled their mindset and changed my approach.

The best way to get motivated is to be around someone already motivated. If you are spending forty-plus hours a week prospecting and don't like doing it or aren't good at it, why waste another minute of your time? Learn how to love and master your craft or get another job.

Mediocrity breeds minimalism. Minimalism over time will destroy your spirit and make you a victim of your circumstances. Tap into your excellence, find a way to surpass ordinary standards, and watch how your life starts to unfold in a fresh new way.

> **Mediocrity breeds minimalism and makes
> you a victim of your circumstances.**

When Your Faith Is Tested

"You can't talk defeat and expect victory." – Tamara Bunte

> *Watch over your heart with all diligence, for from it flow the
> springs of life.* (Proverbs 4:23)

Whatever your heart is filled with your lips will overflow with. You must guard your heart, which means you must be on guard to what you allow your thoughts to think about. This ultimately means you must control your environment. It doesn't matter how motivated you are or how strong willed you can be, your imagination is stronger than your will. If you allow negative people, environments, and words to enter into your consciousness, they will remain. That's why watching horror movies is so bad. It may seem silly or entertaining at the time, but the pictures of what you watch will be held in your subconscious mind. To guard your heart, you must guard your thoughts. In order to guard your thoughts, you **must** consciously choose your friends, what movies you watch, and what environments you enter.

> *He who walks with wise men will be wise, but the companion of fools will suffer harm.* (Proverbs 13:20)

If you want to be good at tennis, associate with people that are good at tennis. If you want to find wealthy business professionals, work in the lounge of a five-star hotel. Have you ever noticed that broke people hang out with broke people?

It's easy to give when you have a surplus of funds. It's easy to be nice to nice people. It's equally as easy to be nice to mean people when you haven't been the victim of an offense. However, what if you are doing what God wants you to do, what if you're living for him and living his way, doing the right thing, but then someone does you wrong or steals from you or turns the people that are supposed to be for you against you?

What happens when life isn't fair, when the shady sales guy takes an account from you, gets away with it, and prospers because of it? At one point or another we all get tested. In fact, the Bible clearly states that we will be tested, but how do we pass the test and remain strong in godliness and escape the corruption of the world?

When your faith is tested, when you are the victim of someone else's bad choices and you wonder where God is, you will have to make a choice. Will you remain bitter, angry, and plotting plans of revenge in your mind? How long will you allow the mistakes and bad choices of others to keep your blood boiling? Winning in the name of Jesus means losing your right to get even, to seek revenge in your heart, to lose the right to pray for harm for that person, and to lose the pleasure of basking in joy when they eventually do fall. To win for Jesus, you have to forgive and let them walk.

Let Them Walk

Below is an excerpt from Steve's Gilliland's book *Making a Difference.* I believe you will find it as helpful in this area as I did.

"The hardest part of turning the page is concerning people. People who were a part of your past and when the challenging times materialized ostensibly vanished. People you treated like relatives and considered as friends simply walked out of your life to go a different direction. I would have never predicted that certain people would have walked away from me. The struggle I had was letting them walk. My counselor, Herb, always said,

'Don't try to talk your wife into staying with you, loving you, calling you, caring about you, coming to see you, staying attached to you. If she can walk away from you, let her walk. Your destiny will not be tied to anyone who is willing to walk out of your life.' The Bible says, 'They came out from us that it might be made manifest that they were not for us. For had they been of us, no doubt they would have continued with us.'" (1 John 2:19)

Your destiny will not be tied to anyone
who is willing to walk out of your life.

It doesn't mean that such people are bad persons. It just means that their part in the story is over. The rough part is the ability to comprehend when a person's part in your story is over so you don't keep trying to revive something that is departed forever. You've got to know when it's over. It took me a long time to acquire the gift of good-bye. I know whatever God means for me to have He'll give it to me. If it takes too much fret and worry, I usually don't need it. The day I officially started turning the page in my life was the day I stopped petitioning people to stay and simply let them go!

I listen to Joyce Meyer every night and have always wondered how, after being abused as a young girl, she could have such a strong faith. So, I went to her website and submitted that very question. "I want Joyce to tell me in one of her podcasts how she can have such a strong faith when she prayed for God to help her and he didn't. How can we trust Jesus when clearly he is going to do what he wants to do?" She answered my question! I would invite you to listen to the podcast "Enjoy your journey-part 2." She addresses how she felt forsaken by God, but how God brought her through it and she came out stronger!

Deceit is in the heart of those who devise evil, but counselors of peace have joy. (Proverbs 12:20)

Steve Gilliland would say turn the page on your bitterness, turn the page on your pain, and decide what's in your story in the next page of your life. Learn from the past so you can live in the good future. You must take the high road. No, it's not easy, but it's worth it. Riding your bike uphill is hard, riding down is easy. It's easy to be angry and bitter. It's hard to forgive, but you end up in much better shape.

Let us run the race with persistence. The reward is there for our taking. We must persist through the pain and the valley of rejection, but once we do we will sit at the top of the mountain. We will be rewarded, we will "Be Skillful," and we will have become the best version of ourselves.

Wisdom from the Pro-Verbs

▸ Success is not always about knowing more, it's about being in a resourceful state of mind.

▸ You attract what your belief system supports.

▸ Don't worry about the haters. They are just angry because the truth you speak contradicts the lie they live.

▸ Let God take on the hurts and injustices, and realize every setback is a setup for something better.

▸ It's true that people don't care how much you know until they know how much you care.

▸ Mediocrity breeds minimalism and makes you a victim of your circumstances.

▸ "You can't talk defeat and expect victory." – Tamara Bunte

▸ Your destiny will not be tied to anyone who is willing to walk out of your life.

Ask Yourself...

Is it time to write a new story?

Is it time to make new friends?

Am I surrounding myself with people that challenge me or cheat me out of my destiny?

In what area of my life am I just doing the bare minimum?

What must I believe in order to fall in love with what I currently despise?

Am I willing to turn the page on my pain and decide what's on the next page of my life?

Pro-Verb Action Steps:

The best way to identify where you are is to take a piece of paper and draw a line in the center, horizontally. This represents your energy line.

At the top of the page write the word "Empowered" and on the bottom of the page write the word "Disempowered."

Now take the eight key areas of your life and decide where they belong on your page. If you feel empowered in a particular area of your life, put that word above the line. If you feel disempowered, put that below the energy line.

- *Life Purpose (what drives you)*
- *Personal Relationship (parents, spouse, etc.)*
- *Business Relationships*
- *Health*
- *Mental Expertise (intelligence)*
- *Financial Wealth*
- *Leadership (people follow you)*
- *Vocation (how much work and how much money you get from your time/energy ratio)*

If you have any of these listed below your energy line, it may mean that you have a limiting belief holding you back from becoming the best version of yourself.

Dig deep and discover what is holding you back.

If you wish to take the Emotional Intelligence Assessment, contact me at www.TamaraBunte.com.

Use the "changing a belief" folder system to start changing your reality.

Imagine you have a folder on your desktop computer on the left side of your screen. The folder is called "Things I no longer believe."

In your mind, place a picture that represents something you no longer believe on the cover of that folder.

Picture yourself typing it up and dragging anything you no longer believe into that folder.

On the right side of your screen, create a new folder that says "Things I know to be true."

Think of something you know to be true, something that no one can take away from you, and use that as the picture for this folder.

Every time you have a new empowering belief come up, type it up and drag it into that folder.

You can take this a step further and imagine someone that you view as successful.

Imagine stepping into that person and borrowing from them their beliefs and modeling their energy. Match your frequency to theirs and live out of this new-found frequency in your own life.

Watch how fast your life starts to change when you change your mindset.

Finally, be strong in the Lord and in his mighty power. Put on the full armor of God, so that you can take your stand against the devil's schemes. **For our struggle is not against flesh and blood, but against the rulers, against the authorities, against the powers of this dark world and against the spiritual forces of evil in the heavenly realms.** *Therefore, put on the full armor of God, so that when the day of evil comes, you may be able to stand your ground, and after you have done everything, to stand. Stand firm then, with the belt of truth buckled around your waist, with the breastplate of righteousness in place, and with your feet fitted with the readiness that comes from the gospel of peace. In addition to all this, take up the shield of faith, with which you can extinguish all the flaming arrows of the evil one. Take the helmet of salvation and the sword of the Spirit, which is the word of God.* (Ephesians 6:10-17)

Conclusion

Sales/Operations Manual – Best Practices for Every Business

He who walks in integrity and with moral character walks securely, but he who takes a crooked way will be discovered and punished. (Proverbs 10:9 AMP)

What are the shared qualities of top sellers?

The Harvard Business School did a study to determine the common characteristics of top salespeople. The evidence they found shows us clearly that most people can be top sellers if they are willing to study, concentrate, and focus on their performance.

Here are the attributes the study found in highly successful salespeople:

▸ ***Did not take "no" personally** and allow it to make them feel like a failure. They have high enough levels of confidence or self-esteem, so, although they may be disappointed, they are not devastated.

▸ ***100% acceptance of responsibility for results**. They didn't blame the economy, the competition, or their company for dips in closings. Instead, the worse things were the harder they worked to make negatives work to their advantage.

▸ ***Above average ambition and desire to succeed.** This is a key area because it affected priorities and how they spent their time on and off the job, with whom they associated, etc.

▸ ***High levels of empathy.** The ability to put themselves in the customer's shoes, imagine needs and concerns, and respond appropriately. All this was a habit for the successful salesperson.

▸ ***Intensely goal-oriented.** Always knowing what they were going after and how much progress they were making, therefore keeping distractions from sidetracking them.

▸ ***Above-average will power and determination.** No matter how tempted they were to give up, they persisted toward their goals. Self-discipline was a key.

▸ ***Impeccably honest with self and the customer.** No matter what the temptation to fudge, these people resisted and gained the ongoing trust of customers.

▸ ***Ability to approach strangers even when it is uncomfortable.**

"Hard work alone will accomplish remarkable results. But hard work with a method and system will perform seeming miracles. No one can profit more by a realization of these truths than the person who sells for a living."
– W.C Holman

The 5-Step Sales Process

1. **Establish Rapport:** Remember, people who are like each other tend to like each other. Match and Mirror:
   ▸ Physiology
   ▸ Tone of voice
   ▸ Representational System (visual, auditory, kinesthetic)

- ▸ Breathing
- ▸ Key words

2. Ask Questions: The questions you ask are directly related to the business of the person you are interviewing. Talk their language. Ask questions in the language of their main interest. In business, talk the language of their business.
- ▸ Find out the client's dominate representation system.
- ▸ Find out the client's buying strategy.
- ▸ Find out the client's motivation, decision, and reassurance strategies.
- ▸ Elicit values so you learn how to communicate to them.
- ▸ Ask "stump" questions to engage in conversation and establish value.

3. Find a Need (create pain): Establish need and establish value. Propose a solution to the client's problem and then ask "What value do you see in this?" If there is no need, then stop and find another client. There are plenty out there.

Your job at this point is to quickly find as many "no's" as possible. That means that you need to push up against the client enough so that he or she makes a decision right now. "No's" are infinitely better than "I need to think about it. Can you call me back tomorrow?" Most salespeople waste 80 percent of their time on people who buy nothing. If you spend 80 percent of your time on people who are going to buy, then they will spend more with you. You only want "High Probability" clients.

Desire: Desire means having plenty of reasons to like the benefits they'll get if they do buy, and plenty of reasons to feel hurt if they don't buy.

While you are in this step, you can also use:

- **Test close** — Is that something you're interested in or not? (This is the only time you may use the word interested.)
- **Conditional close** — "What value do you see in this _____ or what do you value about _____?" or "Is it fair to say that if we solved this problem then that would be valuable to you?"
- **Yes Pattern** — "Then it would be valuable to you to solve this, wouldn't it?"

4. Link the Need or Value to Your Product or Service

At this point, you propose how your product or service will solve the problem(s) that you uncovered earlier. Make a clear proposal of how, but with as little detail as possible. Only tell the client enough to make it possible for them to purchase.

- "What would happen if _____?"
- "Compared to _____" (Contrast frame)
- "Because _____" People always want to know why.
- Agreement Frame: I appreciate, I agree, I respect that and _____.
- Use strategies if you elicited them.
- Also repeat client's values and key words as you close.

5. Close: Ask for the order!

If yes, future pace and get referrals.

Handle Objections by either:

1. Ignoring them and going to #3

OR

2. Handling Objections and going to #3

> *"Success is going from failure to failure without losing enthusiasm."* – Winston Churchill

The Greatest Manual for Sales Success – Write Your Own!
Sales/Operations Manual – This is your Playbook

Table of Contents:

1. Know Your Company's Vision and Mission Statement
2. 30-Second Commercial/Taglines (non-cheesy) verbal and written (Who are you?)
3. Descriptions of what you sell (offerings) for Cross-Sell/Up-Sell options
4. Goals: Number of dials per day/week/month
5. Daily Must List: Money-producing activity (daily accountability to build momentum)

Selling Materials:

▶ Referral Form
▶ Ask for a Referral Script
▶ Obtain Referral Script
▶ Cold-Call Script
▶ Lead Scripts
▶ List of Objections with Corresponding Retorts
▶ Questioning Process –Stump/Hook Questions

Organization System: (Outlook/Gmail/CRM)

▶ List of Categories (groups) with definitions and number of contacts per category
▶ Specific Script per category group (20 max)
▶ Marketing Campaign per category group (6-month plan)
▶ Follow-up (prospecting) Plan per category group
▶ Accountability System (Scorecard)

Must Haves:

▸ 5 Closers "Testimonies" (list of 5 happy customers for prospects to call and close for you)

▸ 3 Networking groups (Identify at least 3 groups to be a part of)

▸ 2 Parties (Host 2 parties a year for clients and prospects)

▸ 1 Gift (give at least 1 gift per customer per year)

Additional Items:

▸ Sample marketing materials

▸ Getting through the gatekeeper techniques

▸ List of lead-generation activities

▸ 5 custom stories (related to overcoming top 3 objections)

▸ 5 influence-closing techniques

Pulling it all together, this is the list of items you want in order to start to create for your own *Best Practices Manual.* Luck is when preparation and opportunity meet. It's time to set yourself up for success. You will create your own luck. You have all of the tools; now it's about action. Time to pick up that phone, make some new friends, and get moving toward the best possible you!

> *The righteous man who walks in integrity and lives life in accord with his [godly] beliefs — How blessed [happy and spiritually secure] are his children after him [who have his example to follow].* (Proverbs 20:7 AMP)

APPENDIX 1:

My Model of Success – Sample Interview Questions

W hen I worked for Tony Robbins, I wanted to be the best. So, I typed up the interview questions listed below and mailed that list of questions in a huge UPS box to the VP of Sales and the top salesperson. I wanted to know exactly what I had to do to be the #1 salesperson for Tony Robbins. I interviewed both the VP of Sales and the top salesperson for three hours each, and within the first three months I outsold my entire team combined. My colleagues kept asking me what I was doing. I would tell them, but because they didn't invest the time and energy to mastering their craft, they didn't apply what I was doing. If you're going to spend 40-60 hours a week, why not be the very best at what you do? Competition is too tight today. There is no room for mediocre results or just getting by.

My "Model of Success" is _____

Below is a list of questions that I asked my model of success. Make sure your model has the outcome you desire!

- ▶ *What are your top ten must-read books of all time?*
- ▶ *What are you currently reading?*

▸ *What positive messages do you currently give to yourself?*

▸ *Who played a critical role in inspiring you to the top? How did it spur you on?*

▸ *What income bracket shifted your mindset? How?*

▸ *What colleagues/friends inspire you and challenge you to be a better person?*

▸ *What movies are your favorites? Which ones inspire you?*

▸ *What websites should I be aware of?*

▸ *What motivational quotes and poems do you read/hang on your wall?*

▸ *Who are your heroes? Why?*

▸ *What is one impact you want your life to have?*

▸ *What habits have you developed that have helped you become a better version of yourself?*

▸ *What challenges do you face today that you never expected vs. where you were ten years ago?*

▸ *What are the top five things you've learned as a result of starting your own business?*

▸ *As a believer, when was your faith challenged? How did you stay strong in your faith? What makes your faith unwavering?*

▸ *How would you coach a person to see their self-worth/identity in Christ rather than what the world teaches?*

▸ *What is something that you used to hate but have trained yourself to like, or what breakthrough comes to mind?*

▸ *What would be your personal five keys to success?*

▸ *What are two personal and two professional goals you have set for yourself this year?*

▸ *What was one of the most difficult times in your life, and what pulled you through it? What belief? What behavior? What action did you use to turn things around?*

▸ *You have attained the goal I desire. Tell me specifically what you did to believe you could have what you now have and what formed your mindset for success.*

▸ *Did someone challenge you?*

▸ *Did they say something that you never forgot?*

▸ *Who did you model in your youth?*

▸ *Who do you look up to today?*

▸ *What do you do when you get frustrated or off track?*

▸ *What five things specifically would you say I must do to achieve my goal?*

▸ *What system, habit, or plan must I follow?*

▸ *What is the greatest lesson you ever learned?*

▸ *Everyone has a genius. What do you believe yours is?*

▸ *What would it take for someone to fill your shoes?*

▸ *Can you list out your greatest strengths/weaknesses?*

▸ *What breakthroughs are you still wanting/needing to have in business?*

APPENDIX 2:

What Makes a Company Great?

How does a company set themselves up for success?
How do you hire the right talent?
How do you enhance performance?

Have you ever met an executive that has the power to run a sales team, but wouldn't or couldn't pick up the phone and make a cold-call if his/her life depended on it? A true leader will lead by example. In order to get a team working together and to inspire an attitude of enthusiasm for prospecting and intentional growth, a true leader must be willing to go first.

Wouldn't it be great if we could just tell someone to go and make sixty calls a day and set two appointments or tell the person that wants to lose weight to just eat less and workout? Why is it we see only a small percentage of people following these seemingly easy directions to achieve success? To start to get cooperation, you want to start asking instead of telling.

> **The key is to draw out the strategies from
> your team, then benchmark their strategy
> against the company's success structure.**

Ask your team what their individual goals are and coach them through what *they* want to be held accountable to rather than shoving sales numbers down their throats. We must inspire rather than control.

Vision and Mission Statements Are Required for Success

Let your eyes look directly ahead and let your gaze be fixed straight in front of you. (Proverbs 4:25)

We can't really begin the discussion of the Vision and the Mission Statements without first addressing the semantic difference between the two. To distinguish between Vision and Mission in our own work, we have defaulted back to the plain English usage of those words. The simplest way we have found to show that difference in usage is to add the letters "ary" to the end of each word.

Vision-ary or Mission-ary?

A visionary is someone who sees what is possible and who sees the potential. A missionary is someone who carries out that work.

Our favorite example of this is Jesus of Nazareth. Jesus was a **visionary**. He saw the potential, the possibilities for making life better. His **missionaries** carried his work and his words to the world, putting his vision into practice. Your organization's vision is all about what is possible, all about that potential. The mission is what it takes to make that vision come true.

Helen Keller was once asked if there is anything worse than being blind. She replied, "Yes, to have sight but no vision."

Vision Statement: This is the big picture. The word vision means the conception of an image. In a vision statement, you say where it is you want to go.

My company's Vision Statement: _____

Mission Statement: The mission statement flows directly from the vision statement. It is the implementation of the vision and outlines what must happen to realize the vision. It's a "how-we-will-get-there" guide that contains action words and adjectives that modify them.

A good mission statement:

▸ Elicits an emotional, motivational response

▸ States things in the positive

▸ Is simple and brief

▸ Contains "Be" and "Do" statements

▸ Can be experienced daily

▸ Makes you happy

▸ Is fully believed and includes self and others

My company's Mission Statement is:_____

Many times, when I work with an executive team, I hand out a blank 3x5 card and ask each executive to write out the company's vision and mission statements. Sadly, I rarely get the same answers. It is impossible to hit a target that you can't see. It is the leader's responsibility to lead a team to one compelling vision.

Where there is no vision, the people will perish. (Proverbs 29:18)

Once the vision is established, having each individual salesperson define their own goals within a parameter of success is the key to success and carrying out the mission. A salesperson then can set their own goals while abiding by the basic sales metrics. This will make them more likely to succeed in reaching their goals..

Once they have picked which level they will commit to, they need to develop their formula for success and then have their manager hold them accountable to follow the plan. The key is to then measure the results in the first two weeks. If they do not stick to the plan they themselves have developed, it is obvious that they are not fully committed to that income level or goal.

"You cannot solve a problem with the same level of thinking that created it." – Albert Einstein

What Makes a Company Great?

The people! Do you have the right people on board? Once you determine if you have the right people, which is usually determined within the first two weeks of employment, you need to decide what kind of culture you want to create.

In order to make your people truly great, you want to have each salesperson take these steps:

Step #1: Have each person decide what they want and why they want it. Make sure it is in alignment with the company vision and mission.

Step #2: Have each person find a model of success and interview that model.

Step #3: Have them set up their own process to achieve their own desired results.

Show them how to take what works from other people, borrow their ideas, and leave behind what doesn't work for them. You will be developing a great company that will benefit all of those involved!

Sales Guidelines

A sales guideline would be...If you are in outside sales, the typical range of outbound calls per day would be about forty dials (two hours of call time); that is ten dials per thirty minutes, which is what I do with sales professionals. I actually sit down with small groups of salespeople, and we make calls together. If you are in inside sales, one should be making between 80-100 dials a day. This being said, a salesperson then can set their own goals but abiding by the basic sales metrics.

Many times companies will pay me to come in and define, for example, three different levels of success. Option A is $50-70K, Option B $70-100K, and Option C is $100-150K. I will set the specific daily activities and processes for each income category. Then each salesperson will have to pick which level they will commit to. What usually happens is the salesperson will pick the 100-150K category. Next, I will give them the formula for success, but then I will have their manager hold them accountable to follow the plan. Did they *do* the necessary steps daily to get to that income level? If not, then in the first two weeks it is obvious they are not fully committed to that income level.

Contact...

tamarabunte
AMERICA'S #1 SALES COACH

To schedule Tamara to speak at your event, call:

704-247-8333

For more information, go to
www.TamaraBunte.com
www.ProverbsForSelling.com

If I speak with human eloquence and angelic ecstasy but don't love, I'm nothing but the creaking of a rusty gate. If I speak God's Word with power, revealing all his mysteries and making everything plain as day, and if I have faith that says to a mountain, "Jump," and it jumps, but I don't love, I'm nothing. If I give everything I own to the poor and even go to the stake to be burned as a martyr, but I don't love, I've gotten nowhere. So, no matter what I say, what I believe, and what I do, I'm bankrupt without love.
(1 Corinthians 13:1-7, The Message)